100 Ideas for Secondary Teachers

Teachers

Managing Behaviour

Johnnie Young

BLOOMSBURY

Other titles in the 100 Ideas for Secondary Teachers series:

100 Ideas for Secondary Teachers: Outstanding Lessons by Ross Morrison McGill

100 Ideas for Secondary Teachers: Gifted and Talented by John Senior

Other Secondary titles from Bloomsbury Education:

How to Survive your First Year in Teaching by Sue Cowley

Teacher: Mastering the Art and Craft of Teaching by Tom Bennett

Why Are You Shouting at Us? The Dos and Don'ts of Behaviour Management by Phil Beadle and John Murphy

I dedicate this book to my beautiful granddaughter Ophelia Jayne Young, born 27th August, 2013.

Contents

Acknowledgements

I would like to thank my wife Sylvie, whose tireless support has helped me with everything I've ever achieved, including this book. I would also like to thank Peter Haddon from Thurstable School and Tanya Wright from Mersea Island School whose cooperation and support have greatly assisted me with this book. Holly Gardner and Ellen Grace have helped me enormously with their professional skills of editing all the way through this project. To the student teachers who have attended my Behaviour Management training courses over the years, I would like to thank you also for your positive feedback of my training which has helped me learn more and more about this fascinating and crucial area of teaching. Thank you all.

Introduction

When I started teaching 22 years ago I found myself returning home every night exhausted and disheartened. I planned to leave the profession because I couldn't handle the behaviour of many of the challenging students. I tried shouting until my voice was damaged; I tried everything I could think of but eventually I had to admit that the dream of being a teacher that I had maintained for so many years while working in business quickly became an empty illusion.

But then I asked myself a question. Why was it that some teachers seemed to be able to manage behaviour so well while others struggled? I realised that the teachers who were good at managing their classes had learnt certain skills that they could use every day. I began to observe these teachers at work and started taking notes about things they did which might be useful to me.

I found that my own classroom management began to improve little by little as I experimented with and adapted best practice and tried out new ideas of my own. I included the best of my ideas in *100 Ideas for Managing Behaviour* (2005) which was updated as *100+ Ideas for Managing Behaviour* in 2007. In 2011, I added to these ideas in *100 Completely New Ideas for Managing Behaviour*. This present book is an updated collection of the best ideas from all of these books, with all of the ideas focussed towards secondary teachers and I really hope that it will assist you in your desire to be a great teacher.

Please try out each idea but also always actively look for ways to improve your behaviour management skills. At the end of each of your lessons make it a habit to think how you could make your lessons even better next time and then take action in small steps to achieve it. You will find that your students enjoy your lessons more and that they learn more. You too will enjoy what you do as you become more expert at it.

Go on, start the next step to becoming a great teacher. I would wish you luck but once you have mastered the craft of behaviour management, luck will have very little to do with your success!

How to use this book

This book includes quick, easy, practical ideas for you to dip in and out of, in order to help you manage behaviour in the secondary classroom.

Each idea includes:

- A catchy title, easy to refer to and share with your colleagues.
- A quote from a teacher or student describing their experiences of using the idea.
- A summary of the idea in bold, making it easy to flick through the book and identify an idea you want to use at a glance.
- A step-by-step guide to implementing the idea.

Each idea also includes one or more of the following:

Teaching tip

Some extra advice on how or how not to run the activity or put the strategy into practice.

Taking it further

Ideas and advice for how to extend the idea or develop it further.

Bonus idea ★

There are 16 bonus ideas in this book that are extra exciting and extra original.

Share how you use these ideas in the classroom and find out what other teachers have done using **#100ideas.**

Phrases to engage attention

"After years of teaching I find that I focus much less on what I'm saying and much more on how I'm saying it."

By thinking carefully about language and using words and phrases in a certain way you will develop effective ways of getting attention in your classroom.

Just speaking to a class with challenging behaviour is often received with low levels of attention. You have to find ways to say what you want to say in a way that will get them listening. I have found that students take more notice of certain phrases than others. They act as strong signals for attention. Here are a few examples that have worked well for me over the years:

- To get attention, hold up an object and say: 'Can anyone tell me what this is?'
- To warn that a sanction is about to be given: 'Right, I don't usually have to do this but you leave me no choice!'
- To get more hands up in response to a question, rather than calling out: 'Come on, only three people can answer this? Surely not! Come on, let's have some more!'
- To quieten a class: 'I'm asking you all politely.'
- To get the noise level down: 'I would like the general noise level down. Five, four, three, two, one...' (Numbers said quickly and sharply then pause).
- To give important information: 'By the way, do you all know about the new system for...?'
- To add important information: 'I nearly forgot to tell you, please don't forget...'
- To urge students to do their homework: 'Danger! (pause) Yes, you'll be in danger of not getting your homework done if you don't tackle it on the day it's given to you.'

Teaching tip

Of course it's not just the words you say that are important, but the tone, body language and attitude that you use to manage behaviour in your lessons. Take note of what works well in your classes so that you can use it again and develop it.

The crucial beginning

"I don't like the beginning of the lesson. I just can't get their attention so I just give the work out and tell them to get on with it!"

With challenging groups, getting and holding their attention at the start is a major challenge and this idea helps at this crucial stage.

Type out what you are going to say (make sure you keep it brief) and hand a copy to each student explaining: 'I want to read you something quickly right now. I'm going to stop and ask one of you, at random, what the next word is. See if you can spot it!'

Start reading, pause dramatically and ask someone who you are sure is following to read the next word. Then say: 'Excellent, you are following. Now let's check that everyone else is!' Read on, choose someone else who is definitely following, give a hearty well done and read on again. You will find that this holds attention much more than just trying to talk at the class.

To enhance the idea:

- Make sure that the student says only one word in response to the question, 'What is the next word please Harry?'
- If they try to read on, stop them and say, in a friendly way: 'I want to read the links just for now and you'll get a chance to read a bit more later.' That way you keep control of the pace at this important stage.
- If you can make the instructions into an entertaining story it holds attention even more effectively.
- Adding an interesting picture helps too.

Scan the noise down

"I spent a long time yelling and stressing before I realised that a quiet and determined scan is much more effective."

If a class is working too loudly and you can't get them to be quiet, 'scan' the room to get the noise level down.

A teacher, in an attempt to quieten a noisy class will often reprimand individual students, shout, bang on the table and nag. But what if those techniques don't work? In practice, the noise level drops initially, but it is soon back up to high levels again and the teacher gets that horrible feeling that it's him or her versus the whole class. So what do you do? I have found that a developed, strategic scan saves energy and works wonders.

- Stand in a prominent position in the room and don't speak, just watch.
- If a student asks you for help with the work or anything say: 'I can't help you until the class is settled.' This is a crucial point.
- Identify the hotspots in the room where most of the noise is coming from. Take your time.
- Start making targeted, firm but friendly reprimand comments, for example, 'Shannon, settle down and get on with your work please.'
- Add strategic praise comments, for example, 'Excellent Jade, you're working well.'
- Continue this process but keep watching the whole class and deflecting any individual requests for help.
- Now start saying: 'Noise lower please. Lower, thank you. Lower. Thank you. That's good.'
- Stand, watch and wait. Keep your whole focus on the noise level.
- Praise the whole class as the noise level falls.

Teaching tip

Keep the focus on the class as a whole, do not get into arguments with individuals and do not insist on absolute silence as it is very hard to maintain and quite unnecessary.

Reduce tension and anxiety

"In the morning I was nice and calm and happy but by the end of a meeting in my department that afternoon I was full of tension and worry, thinking 'how will I ever get all this work done?'"

Get out of the bad habit of working in a tense and anxious way, and therefore be happier and more effective.

Teaching tip

Many teachers in my training sessions have said that talking about relaxing is all very well but with the ever-increasing demands made of them how can they not feel tense? My advice is to make the checklist items on the following page a priority. Start with an image of yourself as calm, relaxed and in control and work back from that point. Be absolutely determined to maintain that state and tell yourself that the main objective of the lesson is to remain calm and pleasant.

The biggest problem I have observed with most teachers is that they are too tense too often. Excessive tension drains the energy levels and exacerbates poor behaviour. A tense teacher encourages a tense class.

Symptoms of excessive tension include:

- Talking too fast (the students will not take it in).
- Over-reacting to minor misbehaviour.
- Forgetting to pause for take up time in instructions and explanations.
- Unnecessary urgency when helping individuals.

I have noticed with dismay that schools themselves are places of ever-increasing tension. The message that this gives students is that tension and anxiety is acceptable and normal.

It doesn't have to be that way. Maintain a pocket reminder checklist, read it before every lesson and act on it until it becomes a way of life for you. Bad habits create tense teachers and these can be replaced by good habits which can create calm, aware and friendly teachers.

The checklist is as follows:

- Just before the lesson clear your mind, even if it's only for 30 seconds.
- Slow your breathing and clench and relax your hands a few times.
- Picture yourself talking calmly, moving calmly, working calmly.
- Remember, when a student asks a question to listen, concentrate and think. Don't rush an answer. Make the answer nice and pleasant to listen to.
- Allow spaces between different parts of the lesson. Encourage quiet thinking time. Pause when talking.
- Develop a relaxed look and smile a lot.

The benefits of using this checklist are:

- You will feel better and enjoy the lesson rather than worrying about what happens next.
- Your students will behave differently.
- The quality of the learning and understanding will be greatly enhanced.
- You will not feel so exhausted.

A lesson in humour

"Without humour it is as if the teacher is a carriage without springs and the students are the heavy passengers. Every little jolt in the road is felt."

The classroom is very prone to stress and tension. The careful use of humour can help make your working environment a more pleasant place to be.

Using humour is a great way to deal with students and can lead to a smoother lesson. However, there are a couple of things to watch out for:

1 Don't use humour until you are confident that you have control over your class. Misplaced humour can cause the very trouble you want to avoid.
2 Be aware that although it may not show, particularly with badly behaved students, they are at a very sensitive and self-conscious age. An inappropriate comment designed to create a harmless giggle could have a really disastrous set of consequences, so never make a personal comment about a student, even in jest, and stick to either making fun of yourself or the topic you're studying.
3 Once you've had a joke or a laugh try and get the class back to the task at hand as soon as possible. The key is to make sure that you keep the momentum of the lesson going.
4 An experienced teacher's use of humour is not so much the telling of jokes but rather a predominant attitude to see the funny side of things. Little good-humoured comments can create a warm classroom environment which decreases the likelihood of confrontation.

Teaching tip

By arrangement, visit a wide range of lessons and have as your focus how other teachers use humour. You will learn a great deal and these methods can be adapted and used in your own teaching.

Taking it further

Show a cartoon or a funny picture at the end of the lesson that links in with and becomes part of the plenary. This is a very upbeat way to end the lesson.

You are in charge

"I don't understand it; I'm friendly enough with them but all they seem to do is take advantage."

Position yourself as a helpful professional who facilitates your students' learning rather than attempting to be their friend.

There can be a tendency, particularly with new teachers, to act too 'matey' with students. This is natural because as adults we are friendly towards each other to ensure smooth working relationships (aren't we?). It is also natural to assume that by being friendly with students they will respond accordingly and you will get the best out of them. But you must remember: you are not their friend; you are their teacher. Your task is to take the lead and help organise and design the best learning environment for them. If you are too friendly students may take advantage of the situation and not do as you ask them. Many challenging students will see your friendliness as a weakness and will try to take control.

As a teacher, you are attempting to build a long-term relationship with your students, where each time you meet with them you help them to learn more and more; it is not just one lesson you need to think about. In order to construct this relationship you must:

- Always be consistent.
- Always be enthusiastic and upbeat (even when you don't feel like it).
- Always uphold the rules.
- Always show interest in their progress.

More than anything you must develop that unique relationship where you are neither a parent, nor a friend but a teacher. Never forget that you are in charge and in the end they must do what you say.

Set up your systems

"Since I have set up and maintained routines my role has switched from reacting to everything to managing and supervising everything; I have so much more time and energy."

Many teachers have such busy schedules that they have little time and energy left to deal with the unexpected but important behaviour issues.

In the management of behaviour never leave anything to chance. Have a system and method to tackle all the core repeated activities. Routines and methods are a great asset to you and will do most of the work for you. For example, have a carefully worked-out routine for:

- Students entering and leaving your room.
- Giving out and collecting in materials and work.
- The structure and use of time in the lesson.
- Setting and collecting homework and dealing with missing homework.
- Marking books.
- Managing rewards.
- Dealing with a student if their uniform doesn't comply to minimum standards.
- Requests to leave the room during a lesson, for example to go to the toilet or see the nurse.

By setting up systems and routines to deal with the foreseeable activities your time is freed up to deal with the unforseeable ones. In my experience as an observer, I have noticed that a great deal of behaviour management problems can be traced back to the simple fact that the teacher is working without effective systems and routines.

Teaching tip

Allow time to check out what other effective and experienced teachers do with their routines and adapt and use them in your classroom.

Bonus idea ★

Implement an 'open book' system. Have a large, clear, simple chart on the wall to showing the main routines in use in your classroom. By regularly referring to it you create a great impression that you are on top of everything. Like all good management techniques, 90% of getting your students to do things is to convince them that you will be checking that they do it.

The 'you choose' technique

"I'm spending most of my time following up incident reports and detentions. I haven't got time to prepare my lessons properly."

The 'you choose' technique uses minimal time and effort to produce maximum effect for reprimands.

It is vital that a teacher is skilful at reprimanding. An effective, time-saving way to do this is to keep the student back after the lesson, call in another teacher to witness the conversation and offer them a choice: 'I can speak to you for one minute now or I can arrange to involve senior staff and that will involve a lot of time, letters home and detentions. We could get this matter sorted here and now if you want to. It's up to you; you choose.'

Explain clearly what it is you are not happy with and what your expectations are for next time. Remember, as always, to show warmth for the student but annoyance at their poor behaviour.

Make a note in your notebook and say: 'I'm going to quickly jot this down here and if your behaviour improves next lesson, as I'm sure it will, then I will cross this out. Now that's fair isn't it? And it will save you a lot of time and trouble.' It is important to be clear about what will happen if the behaviour does not improve and that you will be forced to take it further.

In the next lesson, remind the student to behave and congratulate him or her for the slightest improvement. If they misbehave again then you must carry out the consequences as outlined when you gave the first warning.

> **Teaching tip**
>
> Students with challenging behaviours will have a whole range of convincing reasons why they cannot spare even a minute after the lesson. They will be quite expert at convincing you that they must dash off. That is why it is important to have another adult with you for the one-minute reprimand. If the student still rushes off, it is important that a senior member of staff contacts him or her that day or this idea will not work.

Guard your voice

"The teacher just keeps on talking. I haven't got a clue what she's on about!"

The less you talk and the more they do the better.

As a teacher, your greatest asset is your voice and you must do everything you can to protect it. It is well known that teachers should hardly ever shout, but you should also be aware of excessive talking. Most teachers talk far too much and eventually the sound of their voice becomes background noise to the students. A lot of teachers mistakenly think that teaching is talking so they talk all the time. Talking should be only a part of the teaching process.

For great behaviour management the less you say and the more your students work, the better. You must set things up in such a way as to achieve that goal. It took me years to realise that. If you talk too much, then what you say loses its effect. What's more, it tires you and strains your vocal chords.

You should organise your classes so that the necessity to talk is minimised. Some teachers stand in front of their class and talk for nearly the whole lesson. Look at the students and you will see them in a passive, docile, unresponsive state. They are resting. They are not learning.

Observe a great teacher and you will see the students actively working and the teacher circulating, watching, commenting, guiding, pointing out things and above all asking questions and listening. By listening to responses she will be able to gauge where the students are with their understanding. Her actual talking will be minimal.

Star of the match

"I had a great day today at school. I was star of the match!"

Motivate your students by choosing a 'star of the match' in each lesson.

A great way to motivate your students and make your lesson fun is have a 'star of the match' system. Each lesson, tell your students that you're going to pick a 'star'. You award the title based on a number of different good behaviour or good work qualities that you see in the students:

- effort
- quality of work
- improvements
- perseverance
- good questions asked
- behaviour
- politeness.

State clearly what the star is awarded for and make sure that the whole class knows what they need to do to be chosen as the star in the next class. When you announce the winner make sure you acknowledge lots of other good work seen and stress the range of things you're looking out for in order to include and encourage everyone along. For example, 'Zak you're presentation was great. Martine, I noticed that you got involved with the teamwork today too, well done! And George, the questions you asked were really good and thoughtful. I saw so much good work today, however, I can only choose one...and today's star of the match is Molly! She really stuck with the task even though it was very hard. Well done Molly!'

Teaching tip

As students can get quite competitive, wait until the end of the lesson to announce who the winner is. This way you will avoid any disputes or arguement.

Taking it further

Do all you can to raise the status of these awards to increase the value that your students place on winning them. For example, have small certificates on a display board in your room to celebrate the various stars of the match; send postcards home for parents and carers of winners to see; when visitors and other teachers come to your room draw attention to the stars of the match posters and highlight the students' achievements.

Behaviour notebook

"I used to think that I was weak teacher if I couldn't solve everything there and then in the classroom. Now I see it differently."

Most problems can be sorted out in the classroom but for some it is better to have a long-term approach.

Teaching tip

The advantage of having a good follow up system is not only that it gives you breathing space to think about the problem but it also allows you to have time on a one to one conversation with them, outside of the classroom, to build a better relationship with the most challenging students. I find that you can take this opportunity to show concern, care and interest in them. Jot things they say down in your notebook and ask questions like: 'How do you think we could solve this problem?' When they answer, listen intently and jot what they say down. This, in itself, is a very powerful technique for getting them on your side because it is a way of showing that you care about them.

Teachers often feel under pressure to provide a solution to all classroom problems on the spot. Although many problems can be sorted out straightaway, there are certain things that cannot be. This is where a notebook can be a great benefit.

Take the following example: A student is being deliberately and continually antagonistic. You have carried out the normal reprimands but her behaviour remains unchanged. There is a natural desire on the part of the teacher to react very sternly in an attempt to solve this problem once and for all. But, it might be better to take a longer term approach and say: 'Lily, I have asked you several times to stop antagonising other students and you have completely ignored me. I don't want to get into an argument with you. This is want I'm going to do...' Take out the notebook. Then say: 'I'm going to arrange a meeting with your head of year so that we can discuss what we can do about this. We can't carry on like this.' Make a very brief note in your book and say: 'Now, I must get on with the lesson.' Move away from the student and proceed with the lesson.

The fact that the event is written down, coupled with your quiet, determined attitude to sort it out later has a powerful impact on most students and just carrying out this process can often help solve the problem. The technique will also avoid an argument and show the whole class that poor behaviour is not ignored.

Positive language

"It took me years to realise that the words I used and how I used them shaped entirely the way my students responded to me."

One of the great discoveries every good teacher makes is the importance of the careful use of language. Always think of the outcome you desire and think carefully about how you can phrase any instruction in a positive way.

Creating an encouraging and positive atmosphere must always be the prime objective of your lesson, whatever it is you are teaching. Think carefully about how you say things. For example, instead of saying: 'I told you to be quiet, now I'm getting annoyed!', try saying: 'Excellent. Most of you are settling down nicely. Just a few more and we're there.' Don't say: 'Harrison, no homework again? You never do any homework. You're in detention!', try saying: 'It seems that we have a problem getting you to do homework Harrison, so we'll have a chat to see what we can do to solve this. You work so well in the classroom. Don't worry, I know we will find a solution!'

This approach anticipates the results you require and produces a positive atmosphere. You can adapt it to any instruction and to any kind of behaviour. Your tone of voice may be firm but the underlying message is saying loudly and clearly: 'Things are going well. Keep it up!' Of course, it's not just the words you use that are important, but the tone of voice, the pace, the volume and the body language. With practice these elements will combine to produce a powerful, positive mode of communication.

Teaching tip

Seek out the most positive upbeat communicators at your school and watch them at work. Arrange for them to observe you and give you feedback on how positive they think your language is and how it could be improved.

Bonus idea ★

Arrange a regular meeting with positive teachers and run through some role plays (they are great fun) of various 'what if' behaviour situations to experiment with how best to tackle them using positive language.

Body language

"I began to realise more and more that the less you say and the more you communicate with sheer body language, the more effective you can be."

Develop and enhance your body language to help reinforce your presence in the classroom.

Teaching tip

Arrange to have yourself filmed while you teach so that you can analyse and improve your delivery and body language.

In a classroom, effective use of body language is vital. From the moment you enter the classroom you are under scrutiny; the students are watching you and looking for clues, which they pick up from your body language, so remember:

- Stand up straight; do not hunch your shoulders.
- Show that you are aware of what is going on by broadcasting occasional examples of your observations (for example, 'Well done Matt, you've made a start.')
- Develop signals to indicate desired actions. For example, a finger to closed lips to indicate quiet; a small tug of your ear to indicate 'listen'.
- Move around the room with confidence.
- Have key records (for example, the seating plan) to hand. Don't get caught out rummaging around in your briefcase when your attention should always be on the class.
- When pointing to visual displays be clear and definite, check that students understand.
- Have a commanding position in the classroom from which you always request the class to listen for important instructions. Eventually just moving to that position will make the class listen.
- Try to develop calm movements; build in quiet pauses; never show stress.
- Remember, if a student misbehaves, very often a facial expression from you will be enough to stop them in their tracks.

Bonus idea ★

Get into the habit of exploring the presentations of great motivational speakers. (There is a huge choice on the internet). You will see how they hold the audience by using the techniques of presentation. Particularly notice their use of body language and how it helps enhance their message. Then try to use these techniques and develop them into your own teaching style.

Student feedback

"I like my teacher because he asks us what we like and then tries to do it."

Find out what works best by asking the most important people: the students themselves!

In teaching there is surprisingly little useful feedback. Yes, there are inspections and observations but the amount of information you get from that compared to the total of what you do is tiny. You may, by chance, hear a student commenting about your teaching, but this isn't reliable.

A really useful way to get meaningful feedback is to design a customer-service style questionnaire and ask your students to fill it in. You may not use it for all classes and you may not want to use it too frequently, however, if used carefully, it can supply you with vital information that would remain, otherwise, completely unknown. Examples of the types of questions you could include in your questionnaire are:

- What do you enjoy best in the lesson?
- What types of task would you like to do more often?
- What tasks and activities do you do in other lessons which you would like to do more of?
- What makes you behave well?
- What causes you to misbehave?

This information will help you to understand the aspects of your lessons that are working and those that aren't. It will also enable you to see which are techniques for behaviour management are more effective.

Teaching tip

If you do use new ideas that students have given you in your teaching remember to tell them, and thank them for their great feedback. This makes the whole process of teaching more of an open book where everyone is part of the process of developing, improving and enjoying great lessons. It shows that you care and that you are willing to listen and respond to the students' needs.

The dreaded cover lesson

"I thought that this lesson would be a skive – it always is when we have a cover lesson. But this one was really good. I want him to teach us again."

Prepare for a cover lesson even more carefully than you would for one of your own lessons and you will find that the investment of effort will be well repaid in the long run.

A lot of teachers dread cover lessons. If there are going to be behaviour problems in any class, it's going to be a cover lesson. But covering other teachers' lessons is an important part of your job as a secondary teacher. After all, some day you will need someone to cover your class.

If you take steps to make yourself more efficient as a cover teacher you will gain certain benefits:

- You will enhance your skills at dealing with difficult behaviour.
- You will turn this dreaded task into an enjoyable experience.
- The students will respect you and know you better.
- You will gain useful and unique insights into other subject areas which will enhance your own teaching.

Some of the problems routinely encountered in a cover lesson include the propensity for an unknown class to play up with a cover teacher; absence of a seating plan (or hard to establish one quickly when you need it); inadequate cover work; not knowing students' names and being unsure about the discipline support back-up system for that particular faculty.

So, how can you make a cover lesson a success?

- Try and find out in advance what lesson you will be covering. Although you will often not know who is off until the day itself, it is surprising how often you can be asked to cover a lesson for a teacher whose absence can be foretold, either through booked absence or because of a known period of sickness.
- Check where the room is, who has the key and how you can find the cover work and materials.
- Try to look at the cover work in advance to allow you to work out how to deliver it.
- Find out the arrangements for each department and faculty regarding the discipline support system.
- Make sure you bring with you a survival package which must include spare pens, paper, board pens, etc.
- If you do not get a seating plan the next best thing is to quickly write one out showing where they are sitting as you do the register. This will give you immediate authority because you will be able to call out their names. Don't rely on the fact that they will give you their names, rather get a reliable looking student to indicate where they are sitting as you call the register.

Bonus idea

Over time, put together a folder of starters for all subjects that can be deployed at a moment's notice if the cover work set is inadequate. The trick is to hand it out in a very confident and business like way and anticipate that the students will get on with the task immediately. You will find that getting the students working on something straight away will reduce the risk of disruption enormously. Make sure the starter is clear, interesting, reasonably easy to do and engages them for quite a while.

Self-assessment for success

"I like checking my own work because it helps me understand what I should be doing. The teacher trusts me."

Getting students to quickly self-assess their own work saves you time and results in higher achievement.

As a rule, the more aware students are that their work is being regularly monitored, the better they will work and the better their behaviour will be.

In practice, teachers tend to be a bit random in the way they check up on their students' work. They may focus on certain students' work but not on others. The obvious reason for this is that there is not enough time for you to personally check everybody's work, every lesson.

Teach students to know how to give their own work a quick overall assessment against a criteria for success so that they can quickly allocate a mark out of ten. Keep it simple. When the time is right, for example, half way through a lesson, announce: 'It's self-assessment time!' Be upbeat and enthusiastic.

Then, call out every student's name and ask for their quick-fire mark and jot down the results. You will find their results to be surprisingly accurate, revealing and self-motivating. It encourages trust and the students like it. It's good for learning because it helps the students focus on their own work and gets them thinking about how to improve in a fun way.

The omniscient teacher

"My teacher notices everything. You can't get away with anything."

The best way to manage challenging behaviour is to not letting it start in the first place. Develop an omniscient presence in the classroom — the students must feel that all poor behaviour will be noticed.

The goal for this idea is that students will, at all times, sense your overseeing, guiding presence. It is your presence that will be a strong deterrent to bad behaviour and at the same time foster good work. You cannot achieve this by using shouting, talking continually and blustering around. Instead use a quiet, thoughtful strategy. Here are some techniques that work well:

- Move into the interior space of the classroom and make quiet comments about the students' work.
- Do a lot of silent standing and watching.
- Make comments which show the students that you know how things are going.
- Comment from various parts of the room, including the back, so that students get used to you being among them.

By a careful combination of lots of little actions you will create an omniscient presence. You will also be in an advantageous position of being able to spot things early and then to move in quietly to settle them down quickly before they escalate. You will be able to create a sense of momentum and pace. You will show that you are aware of what is going on and that you are with them every step of the way. You really will be managing what happens in your classroom.

Teaching tip

'Signpost' your lesson by explaining key points, letting the students know how pleased you are with their work so far and reminding them what the next step is. Again the key thing is to praise the good work they have achieved.

Always have a seating plan

"It's not worth asking this teacher if you can move seat. No way will she let you!"

Maintaining a seating plan is an absolute necessity when dealing with a challenging group.

Teaching tip

If a student needs to be moved for a serious reason then you should make implementing it a big deal. Ask a senior member of staff to come in and announce to the class that the decision has been made to move a student. Make everything very formal. Explain that the head of department has a copy of the revised seating plan. The students will see that further moves will involve a lot of fuss and bother and will be dissuaded from requesting to move seats.

Here are some guidelines for implementing seating plans:

- Make sure that the layout is exactly as you want it.
- Keep the more demanding students apart.
- Make sure that any special educational needs are thought through: for example, a student with poor eyesight will need to be at the front.
- Make sure that the first few lessons are carried out with every student sitting exactly in your seating plan. If it requires senior teacher support to maintain this in the early lessons then so be it, this is a battle that must be won. To allow students to sit where they want is to trade away one of your most powerful advantages from the start. It is better that the uncooperative students are removed from the class than to allow them to sit where they please.
- The students will test the waters and ask to be moved for all sorts of reasons. At all costs resist the request to move seats. If you think, 'Oh well, I suppose it won't hurt to just move Nancy. She behaves well anyway,' then other students will argue: 'You allowed her to move seats, why can't I move? That's not fair!' Before long the students will sit where they please and your authority will have been completely undermined.
- Have typed copies of the seating plan displayed on the walls to give a sense of permanence.

How to super-start a lesson

"The hardest part of the lesson is the start."

To warm up the class at the start of the lesson refer to examples of good work that were completed last lesson.

How do you awaken your students' desire to get started? A great way to do this is to remind them of the really good things they did in the last lesson. In particular, pick out a few names of students who did well and encourage them with the upbeat tone of your voice to do even better today.

Examples of the quick-fire comments you could make:

- 'Meera – well done on completing the written task last lesson. I know you'll do really well again today.'
- 'Jack, you are really starting to use some great 'wow' words – that's brilliant. I want to see more of those!'
- 'Mabel, I had no idea you could write descriptions like the one of the misty lake and the castle. That was really excellent!'

By doing this you create a warmth in the atmosphere which anticipates a good lesson. Many teachers start the lesson with a negative attitude, moaning as soon as they enter the room; I have even seen a teacher writing students' names on the board under the heading 'detentions' as they entered the room. That is a big mistake!

The fact that you can quickly recount specific things from last lesson shows how interested you are in their work and will encourage a positive start to your lesson.

Teaching tip

When you use this 'super-start' technique, make sure that you vary the students you mention each lesson and keep good notes from previous classes that are simple and clear so that you can easily refer to highlights. Mention a whole range of things you're pleased with, from behaviour to goals reached, and use that as a link to introduce new work.

Finding an intriguing angle

"When I started to use this technique I saw that I captured their interest from the start."

Find something interesting and dramatic about your topic and use that to engage interest.

Taking it further

When doing your lesson planning add your own box called 'finding an intriguing angle' to make sure you do it every time as part of your planning. Keep a record of what you've used to re-use and adapt.

How do newspapers make a bland story interesting? They find an 'angle' and amplify that interesting aspect to engage the reader. You too can use this technique to enhance the interest value of your topic.

- To teach about persuasive language, refer to a recent popular TV advert.
- To introduce microwaves in Science hold up an egg and ask: 'If I put this egg into a microwave oven and turned it on, what do you think would happen?'
- Say to the class: 'The punishment for stealing a loaf of bread is to have your hand chopped off!' Then, when they look shocked say: 'Well, that was what things were like 500 years ago in this country...' Then lead into your History lesson.
- For an art class, show a picture of a tree and next to it a painting by Mondrian with its bright colourful boxes. Say: 'Mondrian began his career as an artist drawing trees and ended up painting these shapes. It took 30 years for him to go from one to the other. In our art lesson today we're going to try to do the process in one hour!'
- To teach angles in Maths show a picture of the famous mathematical bridge at Cambridge and ask: 'Can anyone guess what is unusual about this bridge?'

The idea will get you into the habit of looking at your teaching material to find something that will immediately arouse interest.

Lesson sharing

"I enjoyed today's lesson. It was interesting and I knew what I was doing because we did something like it in German the other day."

Borrowing the best teaching ideas from other subject areas, as well as sharing your own, is a great way to enrich your teaching and your colleagues' round the school.

Great teachers, by using a small amount of creativity and imagination can take any content, re-package it and mould it to make it enjoyable and useful to their own subject area.

Make it a habit to regularly chat with teachers from other subject areas to find out what has worked well in their lessons then think about how you could adapt the idea for your lesson.

Put the idea into action, saying to your class: 'I've had a chat with the Geography department and I've heard about how successful that class map was when you all contributed to create a map of the UK. So today, I would like to build up a wall poster map for Maths with you all contributing a bit each to show how certain Maths processes work. What do you think?'

The benefits of this idea are:

- You build up working relationships with colleagues from other subject areas, helping each other.
- You show your students that you care and that you want to create engaging lessons for them.
- The ideas are more likely to work well because they have already been 'road tested'.
- You widen your base of resources and ideas.
- Behaviour improves because students are engaged with fun, familiar work.

Teaching tip

Make sure that you offer and share your best ideas with colleagues too so that the process is not one-sided! Not only will other teachers be delighted to hear your ideas but you can ask for feedback on how to improve your ideas and find out how they worked in the other lessons.

Harness their excess energy

"I don't mess about in his lesson because it's more fun doing the fun stuff he's teaching than fooling around."

By usefully harnessing students' excess energy you can reduce poor behaviour.

A lot of bad behaviour can be linked to students having too much nervous energy which needs to be worked off productively before they will calm down.

An active quiz at the start of a lesson works wonders to harness this energy:

- Divide the class into two groups: 'A' and 'B'.
- Ask for one volunteer from each group to represent their team.
- Ask the volunteer to come up to the front of the class to perform a task in competition with the other group. It is important to make it clear that only students who sit quietly will be chosen to volunteer.
- The volunteer will have one minute to complete the task in competition with the volunteer from the other side.

Tasks they could complete include:

- drawing an object on the board in one minute
- human statues
- add that sum
- crack the code
- spell that word.

If managed carefully, students will have great fun and put to good use that excess energy. Usually, they like the game so much that they plead for more. You can use this to your advantage too, promising another game at the end of the class if they finish the work assigned.

Important announcement

"This idea is so much more effective than just telling them off again."

Reading an important announcement from a senior member of staff has great impact with minimal effort.

A really effective technique is to hold up a large envelope, marked 'IMPORTANT' and show it to the class. Call for silence and tell the class that: 'Mr Smith has asked me to read this important announcement to the whole group.' (Choose a teacher who is widely respected and of course, check with the teacher first).

You may want to use this idea if, for example, many students were chewing last lesson and ignored your requests to stop. The note might read: 'Mr Young has explained to me about the problem with chewing gum. I have asked Mr Young to give me all the names of the students who continue to ignore this important school rule. Signed Mr Smith'. Then continue with your lesson as normal.

The advantages of this idea are:

- You can adapt it to any problem which is causing you trouble.
- It shows dramatically that you do not simply forget serious problems.
- The students see that it is not just you alone trying to enforce the rules but the whole school system.
- It is a powerful way to back up what you say with minimal bother to the senior staff.
- It harnesses the fact that the written word carries more authority than the spoken word.

Teaching tip

Use this idea sparingly for important issues. Keep the note short and adopt a serious attitude when you read it out. Remember to report back the next lesson with something like: 'Mr Smith was pleased that you complied with the rules.'

Taking it further

To reinforce the idea, ask Mr Smith (i.e. the teacher nominated) to occasionally call into your class to say a few words to support you.

The power of a good mystery

"I still remember the mysteries, they were the best thing we ever did in class."

A mystery has the power to arrest attention and draw in even the most challenging class.

If intriguingly presented, a good mystery will always capture attention. You can stop a lot of bad behaviour with this one because it engages students' attention so fully.

Choose a suitable mystery, research it and prepare a few pictures to show students at the start of the lesson. With a little bit of creativity, you can make interesting links with the main body of work which you intend to teach them.

Examples of mysteries include:

- UFOs
- Stonehenge
- Atlantis
- the Marie Celeste.

Start by showing them the picture and talk in such a way as to make it clear that you are intrigued by this mystery. Suggest possible solutions, refer to what others have suggested but repeat that it remains a mystery. Ask the class what they think and as they start to contribute add in more intriguing facts to keep the 'pot bubbling'.

Asking for their ideas and thoughts about the mystery is a great way to get students to participate in the lesson. It really prepares their attention making it easier to lead them into the next part of the lesson. You can also use it as a reward by saying: 'If we can finish this section then we'll return to the mystery at the end of the lesson.'

Who's doing the work?

"I was absolutely exhausted at the end of that lesson. I gave it my all, so it must have been a good lesson, surely?"

Managing behaviour is key, but make sure that the students are working too.

I observed a teacher once who was very popular with the students. When she was in full swing she pointed to things on the flip chart, put on a funny hat to make a point about something and at one stage even danced, to the delight of her students. She would occasionally ask a student a question and in reply to his one word answer would punch the air and shout 'great!'

It was clear that the students' behaviour was fine and the teacher was popular. Despite all this, after the lesson I was left with a sense of unease. The teacher had put on a great show and was in complete control of the class, but had I been a student I would have soon figured out that the chances of me being asked a question were low. All I had to do was sit and watch. At the end of the lesson the teacher was exhausted and I'm certain she assumed that because she worked so hard the lesson would have been a very good one. But how much had the students done and how much had they actually learnt?

The point is that although the class behaved well, the teacher did absolutely all of the work. You want to set up a situation where you are in control, managing behaviour and delivering a good lesson, but where the bulk of the work is actually done by the students. Of course you have to demonstrate your tasks and objectives for the class in an engaging way but the aim of that is to get the students working, not to keep them entertained.

Teaching tip

A really useful thing to do is to analyse your lesson, or get someone to do it for you, and then observe a whole range of lessons with the focus being to analyse the use of time. Answer questions like: 'What proportion of the time was I speaking?'; 'How much of the time were the students independently doing good quality work?'; 'How could the balance be changed?' Questions and information like this really focus your attention on how best to use your time.

Supercharge self-centred learning

"I liked that lesson, I really did. There was no confrontation and everyone was helping each other out. I felt part of a team."

How to create a learning environment where the students really achieve self-centred learning.

Teaching tip

To help things along broadcast comments like 'That's a very interesting question – well done'. Give out help sheets, key information cards and checklists and constantly remind the students to refer to them. This will encourage students to help themselves and teach each other more and more.

As a general rule in teaching, the more that you can move the focus from you talking to the students working, the better it is for both behaviour management and quality of learning. However, with a lot of so-called self-centred learning or group activities you may find that in practice a large proportion of the students hide behind the others in the group.

The best way to create an environment that promotes self-centred learning is to switch from the role of 'teacher' to 'facilitator' and become a 'hub' around which the class may then revolve. You manage the materials and the resources but most importantly you set up a busy atmosphere of enquiry. By broadcasting and sharing student's work you will create a momentum of learning.

For example, encourage and remind students to ask lots of questions. Then enthusiastically say things like: 'This is brilliant! Listen everyone. Isaac has written down the intriguing question 'If I throw the number 4 three times in a row on a dice what is the probability of the next throw being a 4?...And Lauren has already worked out an answer to that question!'

The collective excitement will encourage and draw most students into the activities. They will get a sense of progress and purpose working together.

The power of symbols

"Less is more. Instead of trying to get myself heard above the din, I simply show the symbol. It works like magic!"

To save yourself having to continually repeat routine instructions, train students to instantly recognise and react to symbols that you hold up.

If you set up good routines you avoid using up excess energy because you don't have to keep reminding students about what to do at key points in the lesson. To support and maintain these routines introduce the use of symbols and you will find that everything flows more smoothly. Here are some examples:

- If some students still have their bags on the desk and the rule is to place them out of the way, hold up a large picture of a bag with a large red cross through it.
- If some students haven't taken their homework diary out hold up an enlarged picture of the diary at the appropriate moment.
- If you want students to change activities show an arrow curved like a circle.
- A popular one for listening: a large ear!
- If the noise level is too high show a noise gauge and point to where you want it to go.

Teaching tip

Ensure that the symbol is clear and simple, mounted on an A3 card, and that it is used regularly.

Taking it further

To enhance the idea, when you hold up the symbol, ask one of the group to say what it means and praise them for it. It is another way of making your message clear. When you have a good relationship with the class and they are used to your routines then invite volunteers to come up to the front and hold up the symbol and do the task for you. This helps get away from confrontation and engenders the sense that you are all working together for a common purpose.

Student-monitors

"As a new teacher I concentrated on the content of what should be taught. It didn't occur to me then that the simple things, like giving out and collecting in materials, could cause so much disruption."

The logistics of distributing materials for your lesson is almost always underestimated. You must have, and effectively use, a good system.

Teaching tip

One of the most difficult problems to overcome with the use of monitors is when they refuse to help. Having a rota goes a long way to solving this problem but it will also help if you employ a brisk, no-nonsense approach when you allocate the monitors; it's not a choice. It is also helpful to quietly have a word with the monitors at the start of the lesson to remind them it is their turn today as it puts it in their minds and prevents arguments disrupting the class.

Although it appears straightforward, handing out materials can cause chaos. To minimise disruption make sure you have a carefully worked out system in place.

First, never give out work yourself. It is exhausting and takes away from your primary role of keeping an overview on the class at that critical part of the lesson. Instead, have a rota of student-monitors, recorded on your seating plan, to give out the work for you.

To use monitors effectively:

- Make sure that your monitors have a particular row or group which they distribute to and collect from.
- Insist that your students put their pens down and listen carefully before work is collected.
- Allow plenty of time to collect everything to avoid chaos when the bell goes.

Second, it is vital to explain to the class how you want the work collected, before the monitors get up. 'Finish your work. The green sheet is for your homework. Place the blue sheet at the front of your desk. Now monitors, listen carefully, I want you to collect blue sheets. Did everyone follow that? Right, monitors collect the blue sheets now please.'

Student presenters

"At first I was a bit nervous, but now I love going up and helping the teacher present his lesson. I want to be a teacher!"

Getting the students to assist you and present parts of the lesson works wonders for behaviour management.

The standard model for teaching has always been that the teacher stands at the front of the room and presents information to a group of students. It took me a long time to realise that getting the students to help *me* present is a great thing.

If it's not managed carefully, however, it can result in too many students doing too many things and the result is chaos, scaring the teacher off and causing him or her to revert to traditional methods. But by using method and process, involving students in the presentation can be wonderful for behaviour management.

Ask for volunteers to come up to the board to help you. Give them a board pen each and ask them to write key words as you go through your presentation. Cue them with the key words to help the smooth running. Key words and short phrases work better than lots of writing.

This helps with behaviour management, engaging students, and is more fun because the focus of interest is enhanced. The important thing is to remind the class that you are looking for the next 'quiet' volunteer to come up to help.

Students learn useful note taking skills and later, when you refer to the key words on the board in your teaching, you are again engaging them in the lesson by using their notes.

Teaching tip

When you sum up at the end of the lesson, involve more volunteers to come up and assist you. It is key, whenever you invite new volunteers up to say, for example: 'Thanks you two, that was just right. Now, if you could sit down (take the pens off them at this point) then I can choose a couple more volunteers.' Never have more than two volunteers up at a time.

To teach is to learn twice

"I learn from my friends as well as from the teacher, and I'm not embarrassed to ask stupid questions."

Set up your classroom so that students can teach each other.

The most effective way to learn is to teach someone else what you know. Try to set up your classroom activities so that there are many opportunities for the students to teach each other. It becomes more interesting and dynamic and automatically helps with behaviour management. It also has the following benefits:

- Learning is sharper.
- Confidence is built up.
- Excess energy is harnessed.
- Strain is taken off the teacher.

A note of caution: It is natural to assume that the model is for the brighter student to teach the less able. With imagination you can depart from that model. Try to:

- Organise tasks where students need to get information from each other to complete a task.
- Arrange the resources so that different students get different information.
- Make sure that your role is switched to help the process work smoothly so that students get into the habit of going to each other, rather than to you for answers.

The uninterested student

"How did you get Ben working? He never does anything for me!"

To get the uninterested students engaged, link the work you are setting to work that the student has had success in.

This is a very challenging problem. Some students, despite your best efforts, still have no interest whatsoever in the work you set them. Keep them back for a brief chat. Explain that you've noticed their lack of interest over a series of lessons. Approach them with a genuine spirit of curiosity. The usual response will be that they find the work 'boring'.

With careful conversation you can discover the subjects and areas that do interest them. You may need to persist, but there is always something!

If, for example, they are good at Geography and your subject is English, you could say: 'Ben, I've been thinking about our problem, that you don't find English that interesting. Now, you told me that you like drawing maps. Well how about if you draw a map for me connected to the novel we're reading? I'll show you how you might wish to start it off. Do you want to give it a go?'

The benefits of this approach are:

- The student will see that you are trying to make the work interesting and this will help cooperation.
- You can now comment on improvements seen (however small) and this will help develop the learning relationship.
- You can build on this success to plan the next piece of work.

Teaching tip

Once you have built this important bridge and got your student working you can be active in trying to re-introduce the original work you had in mind for the student. You will have much more chance of success because you have prepared the ground.

Taking it further

When you have found out what your challenging students are interested in, try to tailor the resources you create to their interests. By giving the student something specifically aimed at them they will notice and appreciate the effort you have made to engage their interests.

Never be alone with a student

"She claimed that I said something inappropriate. That's ridiculous! I was explaining her homework to her. Now I've been suspended while it's investigated. This is a nightmare."

You must never allow a situation where you are alone with a student because you must be protected from the risk of false accusations.

Although this is a basic point it is troubling how many teachers ignore it. If you're telling off or praising a student at the end of the lesson when the rest of the class have gone you must always make sure someone else is with you. This is common sense and must not be forgotten. The vast majority of situations will mean that this is unnecessary, but it must be done to protect from the trauma of a false allegation of misconduct.

If a false allegation is made the focus will not so much be on what was done or not done. The first question will be 'Why were you alone with that student?'

Some teachers rely on having another student present but as a general rule I would recommend having another adult present. Once you are in the habit of thinking this way and acting in a cautious way you will find that in practice it is not difficult to arrange.

Teacher-TA partnership

"As a teaching assistant I love to work with the teachers who work with me and share the tasks rather than someone who bosses me around and gets me to do menial tasks."

With a little planning and discussion of rules and guidelines, you and your assistant teacher can create a powerful partnership.

Teaching assistants are fantastic for helping with the management of behaviour. Unfortunately, it's quite common to find that the partnership between teachers and their assistants is nowhere near as effective as it could be. Usually, the assistant is underutilised due to poor communication and the mistaken belief that the teacher is the 'boss' and must always direct the assistant. Rather you should work in partnership.

Here are some guidelines to get the best out of this partnership:

- Meet outside of the classroom to outline strategies and approaches.
- Develop a double act by rehearsing together a set of 'what if' scenarios so that together. The double act is much more interesting and engaging for the students.
- Give your assistant a brief outline of your lesson plan.
- Encourage your assistant to use your full authority and constantly remind your class of this.
- If you have a particularly challenging student, ask your assistant to sit with that student to help them focus.

Teaching tip

If a student is not working, is giggling and disrupting the class, move close to them (but not too close) with your assistant, stand close by. Within earshot, have an informal chat with your assistant where you discuss how disappointed you are with the student's behaviour (the assistant concurs) and how you expected so much more of her, as you know she can behave well and do the work. Then turn to the student and request that she settle down and continue her work. Then you and the assistant must move to other parts of the room. The combined physical presence of two adults discussing the student and being firm, fair and encouraging will have a very powerful effect on the student's behaviour.

Keep students in their seats

"Zak walked past me to sharpen his pencil and dug me in the arm with it, so I tripped him and then we started fighting."

It is important to maintain a system that ensures students stay in their seats.

A huge amount of disruption and more serious problems can be traced back to the teacher allowing students to leave their seats and wander about.

You must enforce the rule of staying in seats all the time. Broadcast to the class reasons why staying in your seat is important and this policy will be much more successful. Say: 'If there are 30 people in a room we must have rules or there will be chaos. So staying in your seats is really important!' Then support the situation by thanking them for their compliance: 'I've noticed that when I ask you to go back to your seats you do so straight away. Thank you for that. Doesn't that make the classroom more settled! Well done!' By giving them a positive, upbeat running commentary it moulds expectations and gets the message across.

If you teach a subject or activity where students need to leave their seats, like art, music, drama, or technology then obviously you will have to let them get up. However, always have a strategy and a clear system in place, watch them and make sure that they comply with it. For example, the rule could be that although they are allowed to move around for the exercise if they mess about rather than do useful activity then they will immediately have to go back to their seat.

Taking it further

Work out the reasons why students commonly try to get out of their seats and be one step ahead. For example:

- If they want to sharpen a pencil, sharpen it for them (or hand them a sharpener that collects the shavings).
- If they need a worksheet or book say: 'I'll bring that to you so that you don't lose your momentum. Stay there please.'

Reframe the conversation

"I used to get into arguments with those 'nothing's right' students. With this technique I can transform the temperature of the conversation and it can often turn out to be a pleasant and useful discussion."

How to take control and reframe a negative conversation.

Imagine this situation. A teacher approaches a student who is obviously unhappy about something. The teacher asks if the student is OK, but the student replies that they hate the school, the teachers, the students – everything. Of course, the teacher offers up reasons to be cheerful, pointing out the new common room but the student sees this as a platform to make even more negative comments about the school. In this case, the teacher is allowing a conversation to take place where the student is given a free rein to speak out with the sole intention of insulting the school and its teachers.

So how do you handle a conversation like that? You must take control of it. Instead of giving positive comments in the hope that he will change his mind, start reframing everything you say by using questions like this: 'What would you like to see here?' and 'How would you make changes to the things that annoy you? Give me some examples please, will you?' The important thing here is to really listen to their suggestions and then start agreeing with parts of his ideas and encourage him to develop any that are genuinely good. Say 'That's a good idea,' or 'I like that one.' This establishes a slice of common ground, which is vital in compromising opposing viewpoints.

Teaching tip

Sometimes the student will still be difficult in his replies to your questions. It is best to persist a little at this stage and say: 'I know you're feeling annoyed, but I'm trying to get to the bottom of this. If you have good suggestions to improve this situation, perhaps I could discuss your ideas with the headteacher.'

Taking it further

If this is a persistent problem at your school, consider setting up a student council to brainstorm ideas about how to tackle and improve the areas that the students complain about.

Rules sound better this way

"This is so effective that half-way through me giving a reason for the rule they just comply! It's a great technique!"

You are much more likely to get students to comply with the rules when you offer a reason for them. Turn the abstract into concrete thinking.

Just telling students that something is simply 'against the rules' is a very cold, abstract and ineffective way of enforcing them. Instead, offer illustrations to dramatise your point.

For example, don't say 'Don't throw pencils please, it's against the rules'. Instead say 'I read in the paper recently about a boy who was blinded in a classroom because another boy threw a pencil at him. So obviously, I'm asking you to put that pencil down now, please.'

You don't have to make all your illustrations quite so dramatic. Supposing, for example, a student has a bag on her desk and the rule states that it should be on the floor under the desk, then try saying, in a friendly way: 'Alice, I've just glimpsed some juicy-looking sweets in your bag so if you pop the bag on the floor you won't be tempted to break the no eating in class rule, will you?'

A common problem is when students interrupt. Try saying: 'I love having discussions with this class, I really do. But, if you don't keep to the rule of one person speaking at a time then I won't be able to hear all your good ideas, will I? Come on now, one person at a time!'

If a student takes another student's property say: 'You know what I'm going to say. Nobody likes it when someone else takes their things. That's why it's such an important rule.'

This habit of reminding students all the time about the reasons for the rules seems to remove the confrontational nature of the communication. It engenders a cooperative and caring atmosphere. Rather than the rules being seen to 'ruin the fun' they can be seen as protecting it.

Bonus idea

Tell students short stories to illustrate rules. A good one is:

'I once had to referee at a child's football game while we waited for the regular referee to arrive. I didn't know what I was doing and the children started playing football. Nobody was sure who was on whose side. Nobody was even sure where the goals were. Arguments broke out over whether the ball was in play or not. More arguments started about who had scored and whether or not it was a goal. Fouls took place unabated and eventually a fight broke out! All of a sudden, a horn sounded and Big Jack, the referee, arrived with all the gear. He stopped the match handed out coloured team bibs, marked out the pitch and established goalposts. He blew his whistle, and with his firm confident presence, the game commenced. So I ask you, which game to you think the children enjoyed the most? The one with the rules or the one without?' Allow a pause for all the information to sink in and then choose someone to answer the question. Allow another pause and say, 'You see, we need rules, and we all need to keep to them, even to have fun.'

Taking it further

Try this technique in other areas of your teaching, for example, when students ask, 'Why do we have to study this?!', give them real life examples for why they will find the topic useful in their life outside the school. 'Being able to write a formal letter will come in handy when you need to apply for a job and write a covering letter'.

Real success for 'low achievers'

"I don't feel like a failure in his class."

How to redefine the meaning of success

Students' poor behaviour is often linked to low ability. You can sense a sort of disabling mood of failure in all they do. This can be made worse by the education system's obsessive focus on high academic results.

I once met a father and his son at a parents' evening. The son's expected grade was 'fail'. By the time the father left, he was laughing, shaking my hand and thanking me and the boy was all respectful smiles. A colleague, who knew the circumstances said to me: 'What on earth did you say to him?' Of course, I had told him the truth, focusing on how good Kieran was at dealing with people and predicted that that skill would be very useful to him in life.

Constantly link success to things outside academia, like effort, thinking skills, asking good questions and being polite. By giving enthusiastic praise when you spot these things you will build students' self-confidence and help them feel good about themselves.

Examples of things to praise:

- Being kind and thoughtful to each other.
- Seeing things from the other person's viewpoint.
- Keeping uniform and appearance smart and tidy.
- Being better organised than last lesson.
- Sticking at a problem and not giving up.
- Thinking creatively about something.

With persistence you will build up a strong belief that results are not the only way to define success.

Comparison is convincing

"He's a fair teacher. He's on my side."

Show comparisons to illustrate improvements in behaviour.

Many teachers, when keeping a student back after a lesson, will ask the student to write down what happened and why. This excellent technique allows the student to offer their side of things in a reflective way.

But the problem is that almost always the student's note will be discarded and that will be the end of it.

If you keep the note, and several lessons later have a quick chat with the student and read the note back to them, it will have a very convincing effect on their behaviour. Point out how pleased you are with the specific improvements now seen.

Examples of how comparisons can be powerfully communicated:

- 'Last lesson you seemed to be yelling out a lot but I'm pleased to see that you put your hand up today, thanks for that. If you can get that even better next lesson we'll really be getting there.'
- 'I noticed that although you are still getting in a bit late you weren't as late as last time, which is great but I'm sure you can get here on time if you put your mind to it.'
- 'Last lesson you only wrote a few lines. Today, almost twice as much! I'm looking forward to next lesson to see how much you'll do then.'

Teaching tip

Try to build up a reputation with your students that when you call them back after a lesson, the chances are it is to praise them rather than reprimand to them.

Taking it further

If you have the time to write a short note of improvement and show it alongside the original note then it gives an even more powerful proof of progress.

Inspirational people

"It's years since I left school but I still remember those amazing people our teacher used to tell us about."

Showing students case studies of inspirational people who have triumphed in the face of adversity has a powerful motivational effect on them.

Students with poor behaviour often feel that they are no good at anything and their low self-esteem creates the firm idea that they won't do well in life. They feel that there is just too much against them. I have found that giving a short inspirational talk about someone who has overcome the odds to achieve success can be highly motivating.

I try to make these talks interesting by showing pictures and presenting the whole thing as a short high-impact story. First, I engage the students in some of the details of the problems the person faced and then I show them how the person triumphed.

Inspirational stories are easy to find in newspapers and magazines when you start looking. Examples of stories include:

- A man who was nearly burnt to death in an accident and now travels the world delivering motivational talks.
- A rugby player who, despite being paralysed in an accident, still coaches rugby.
- A man who achieved no qualifications at school but went on to become a billionaire businessman.

The brilliant break

"I found that allowing my students to enjoy a short break in a lesson is a sensible idea, not only is it very appreciated by the students but it also refreshes their energy."

If given now and again and timed well, a short break can work wonders.

A short break in the middle of a lesson can be extremely effective when managing behaviour but it must be implemented infrequently and it must always be brief. Allow a break too often and students will begin to expect it; allow a break that is too long and it will be impossible to regain their attention. And, of course, only include a break in your lesson plan if you have time.

To use a break in your class, take advantage of a situation where your students have done well. Praise them for their good or efficient work and let them have three minutes to chat quietly while you are preparing for the next task. Once the time is up have a strong signal (for example, a bell ringing) to let them know that the next task is beginning. The students appreciate the goodwill that this creates.

The students must keep to two important conditions for the break to work smoothly:

1 The noise must be kept to a reasonable level.
2 They must agree to pay attention when the lesson recommences.

Playing music during the break works well because it creates a relaxing atmosphere and turning it off is a powerful signal that the break is over.

Teaching tip

It is useful to have a range of quick-fire fun activities, for example, quiz cards, optical illusions or fact books, to hand out to students who may find the break awkward or who might not have anything to occupy them and feel reluctant to chat with peers. This can also control the noise level as students absorbed in the activity are less likely to chat or call out across the room to each other.

Colour coding behaviour

"Even badly-behaved students appreciate some acknowledgement that they're doing better, however slight that improvement may be."

When students realise that their behaviour is being systematically monitored and recorded then there is a powerful innate tendency for that behaviour to improve.

For this idea to work it must be kept simple and followed up in every lesson. Towards the end of the lesson, allocate a behaviour colour to each student. This must be done in a positive and upbeat way. Use four categories, for example:

- Green – excellent.
- Orange – good.
- Blue – satisfactory.
- Yellow – room for improvement.

Sum up quickly towards the end of the lesson (don't forget reminders during the lesson) and say things like:

- 'Darren, you have definitely improved your behaviour today, so I'm pleased to give you orange!'
- 'Wayne, I'm a bit disappointed and you know why. I've got to give you a yellow.'

Follow up by having a large chart on the wall with the students' names clearly displayed down the left hand side. Each lesson colour in the boxes, or use stickers, so that everyone's behaviour and, importantly, progress is there for all to see. You will find that the students will want to earn a good behaviour colour and that they'll compete with each other. Attend to the chart in every lesson and draw attention to it regularly. Explain that copies will go to the head of subject and will be used at parents' evenings. Indeed, individual records can easily be sent home each half term.

Slow down, get the pace right

"The teacher talks so fast, putting stuff up on the screen all over the place. I don't know what he's on about, so I mess about."

You must control your pace during your lessons. Your pace has enormous consequences for the behaviour of your class.

A common problem for teachers is the speed at which they operate in the classroom. It is natural with 30 students demanding your attention to want to respond quickly and resolve all of their problems. But remember that the demand on your time in the lesson will always outstrip your ability to sort everything out. If you do go too fast, in some vain effort to sort everything out, then three things will happen:

1 Students will not be engaged and will misbehave.
2 The quality of your teaching is reduced because of the speed at which it is delivered.
3 You will eventually burn out.

To improve your pace, try the following:

1 Make it a habit to occasionally ask yourself whether you are going too fast.
2 Try to do one task at a time, at a steady pace.
3 Refuse to be interrupted when you are giving individual help.
4 Learn to reduce the quantity and improve the quality of the help you give.
5 Over time, teach your students to understand your method of helping one at a time and about patience; always make sure they have something to do while they wait.

You will have more energy and your students will actually learn more from you. Learning should always be based on a systematic, carefully worked out process rather than a frantic rush to satisfy the chaotic demands of the group.

Teaching tip

Broadcast your method frequently so that students know what is going on. Remind them to work patiently until you can give them individual attention. By slowing the pace you will think more clearly, be less likely to make errors and be empowered to strategically manage the whole class and the situation at all times.

Reintegrating ringleaders

"It is a strange fact that three or four students can spoil a whole group."

The way ringleaders are put back into your class is of crucial importance.

Where troublesome ringleaders have been isolated from your class you must carefully consider your strategy to reintegrate them. Bear in mind the following points:

- Make sure that you have senior management support, either to watch the students settle back in or to call upon for a speedy response if required.
- If a group of troublemakers' behaviour has been extreme try reintegrating one at a time over a series of lessons.

Often, challenging students who regularly disrupt a group will not respond to normal behaviour strategies. When they have been re-introduced into your group there is a danger that their behaviour will quickly deteriorate to where it began. It is crucial, therefore, that they are monitored in some way. Show them that they are on 'probation' before you make a final decision to have them back in your group. Once they are re-integrated, monitoring should take place quietly in short but frequent one-to-one chats with them. Always put the focus on the positive things you have noticed.

Plan the practical stuff

"Why did I spend so much time planning the theoretical content in detail, and give so little thought to what actually happens in my lessons?"

Prioritise behaviour management considerations when planning for a challenging class.

Naturally, teachers plan their work by starting with the syllabus and breaking it all down into a series of lesson plans. Behaviour management concerns are not usually part of this planning process, usually they can be dealt with as and when they arise in the lessons.

But when you have classes with challenging behaviour you must turn the planning process on its head. The best place to start is to consider how your students deal with the actual activities presented to them. For example:

- What works well for them?
- What sorts of things work particularly well at the start of lessons?
- What kinds of activities are likely to cause trouble?
- How can you arrange a smooth flow of work?
- What could you suddenly switch to if things go wrong?

Supposing the lesson plan says: 'Give out cards for the students to match up.' What might happen with all those cards? Will leaving their seats cause trouble? Is there a better way to do the task that reduces the risk of poor behaviour, for example, a worksheet with everything in one place, rather than using cards?

By changing the way you think about planning you will immediately improve the chance of a successful lesson. Be creative in the ways in which you present the information and design the activities.

Teaching tip

Think about the activities that students can already successfully do, or enjoy doing and adapt new lessons around them. When you get into the habit of thinking this way you develop a whole new enhanced way of working.

The golden vision

"If you don't know where you're going, how do you know when you get there?"

Constructing a clear mental vision of what you're trying to achieve will help you to achieve it.

Give your class a vivid picture of what they will have achieved by the end of the lesson. For example, tell the students that: 'By the end of this lesson you will be seated around a table, in groups of four, enjoying an imaginary dinner where you are eating French food and chatting to each other in French. One of you will be a waiter and will be taking orders in a notebook and another will be the chef. I will be the *maître d'* and I will come around to each group to ask you about your meal, in French. Do you get the idea? It will be a bit of fun.'

It helps if you can move around the room and indicate enthusiastically where things will be. When you've set up the structure of the vision start asking for their ideas. For example, ask: 'What do you think we need to do to make sure that only one person speaks at a time?' The students will suggest ideas and basic rules of behaviour management back to you.

Sharing this 'golden vision' of what you want the class to achieve and how you're going to achieve it brings together the abstract content of the lesson and the reasons why good behaviour is so necessary to it. As the class helped you construct the vision there is more chance that they will work harder to get to it because you'll be working with, rather than against, each other.

The instant report

"It's amazing how a piece of paper can hold such authority!"

How to use an official report for maximum compliance.

When trouble emerges in your class and your usual warnings and control mechanisms fail to work, try using an instant report. You will need to have some official headed paper that has 'Headteacher Report for Serious Concern' written in bold at the top.

Make sure that the class is working on something and make your way around the room. This will give you the opportunity to have quiet one-to-one conversations with any troublemakers. To the troublemaker, say something like 'Molly, I'm afraid we have a problem here. Remember when you were shouting at Megan, and you ignored me when I asked you to stop? Well, the headteacher is absolutely insistent that when something as serious as this happens we have to create a report, to give to him straight after this lesson.' Show the student the report, write their name clearly on it and then ask: 'I've got to put a reason on the report. Can you tell me what I should write to explain why you ignored me?'

Then, holding the pen poised to write, use the report as a bargaining tool: 'Look, if you can behave well until the end of the lesson, I'll ask the headteacher if this report can be ignored.' (Don't say that you'll throw it away. You have to emphasise its importance).

The threat of the report is usually enough to stop the problem because very often the problem is that the student doesn't understand that what they've done is serious. The report makes it dramatically clear with minimal effort.

Teaching tip

This idea allows you to almost 'team up' with the student to help them out of a problem. Try to show the student you are on their side and by working together to manage their behaviour the report will not be sent to the headteacher.

Deflective techniques

"He's a good teacher. I don't know why, but you sort of stop mucking about and get on with it."

Use the power of deflective conversation to manage challenging behaviour.

When dealing with students who are challenging in their behaviour it is very important to carefully manage the conversations you have with them.

Students who are used to getting into trouble can become immune to being told off and threatened with sanctions. The key to dealing with such students is to build up long-term relationships based on consistency and trust.

For a technique with immediate effect, try the Strategic Deflective Conversation (SDC) technique. Engage the student on a topic that has nothing to do with the behaviour issue. This will enable you to diffuse a situation before it escalates. For example, 'Henry, your PE teacher told me about your winning goal the other day. Tell me how it happened!' When you've established a rapport lead into the behaviour that you want to address.

This way the behaviour issue is broached informally, and isn't the focus of your conversation. Another example would be: 'I noticed you were getting a bit bored there, Zak. Chucking paper planes about can certainly be a sign of boredom, I tell you what, I'll do my best to make the next bit of the lesson a bit more interesting, but could you do your bit? Could you not throw anymore planes?' Then smile, creating a sense of expectancy and agreement (like a metaphorical handshake), move away and, most importantly, get on with the lesson.

The hands up rule

"Like all training, when everyone is used to the rule then it works well. You have to keep on reminding them about the hands up rule or there will be chaos. My classroom has been much improved by me insisting on this rule."

A lot of success in a classroom depends on a system of turn taking. The traditional 'hands up' rule is still the best one but must be carefully managed.

Insist that the students put their hands up when they wish to ask a question or contribute to discussions.

A common problem is that a student puts up his hand and then speaks anyway. So, it's a good idea to designate times in the lesson when you make it quite clear that you don't want anybody to put their hand up as everybody should be listening at that point. If somebody ignores you and puts up their hand, stop and remind them of the rule. You will find that if you stick to this the students will get used to and comply with your system.

Make it a habit to congratulate students who stick to the protocol and continue to reprimand those who break the rule and you will gradually win the class round.

Teaching tip

Make it clear that you never allow someone to speak if they break the rule for turn taking. If someone shouts out, repeat, like a mantra: 'I don't want you to speak at the moment, because you broke our important rule of turn taking and that is not fair to everyone else.'

Taking it further

It is well worth the time and trouble to make sure that all teachers in your school comply with the hands up rule. How can you enforce a rule that is so basic to success when other teachers are allowing it to be flouted? Certain fundamentals must be rolled out, used and enforced across the school or you are fighting a losing battle. A standardised poster for each room is a good idea.

Tell them off with praise

"My teacher is sort of nice. You do what he says because he isn't horrible to you."

You can get the best behaviour from your students, not by telling them off but by using the powerful language of praise.

When students refuse to work or do not comply with your instructions, teachers often quickly revert to the 'default mode' of telling off. I have found that it is much better to use the language of praise to encourage the students to behave in the way you desire.

By praising the student you can actually get them to comply, get them back to work and keep the mood of the class upbeat.

Ideas of ways to praise instead of telling off include:

- 'Michael, you are the last person I would have thought would interrupt me when I'm in the middle of explaining something to the class. You normally listen so well. [Pause.] You can do better.'
- 'John you've hardly done any work, I'm surprised. Normally, when you understand something you work well on it. Would you like me to explain it to you again?'
- 'Naomi, that is odd. You're quite late and normally there would be a good reason for that. How about settling down now and getting on with the work. At the end of the class we'll have a quick chat and find out what's wrong?'
- 'Dave, that new phone must be a birthday present. However, you know what I'm going to say because you listen. Now, put it away and I'll pretend I haven't seen it so that we can get some great work done!'

Attention-demanding students

"I used to rush round the classroom, answering students who demanded my attention. With these sheets I found that I could help manage their demands and put myself back in control."

How to occupy the few students who constantly demand all your attention, allowing you to deal with the whole class.

A small percentage of students can occupy a huge percentage of a teacher's time and by attending to the ever-urgent needs of the few they neglect the needs of the less demanding majority. How do you solve this age-old problem?

First, explain to the class that you want to be able to go round and see everyone's work. That is only fair. Prepare a worksheet, headed: 'Brain training while you wait'. The purpose of the sheet is to occupy students while you help others.

The selection of the contents of the sheet is important. Adapt these examples to suit your group:

- A place where the student can write down a question about what he doesn't understand.
- A small word search is crossword or Sudoku.
- A simple drawing with a box next to it that says: 'How well can you copy this picture?'
- A set of straightforward general knowledge questions.
- A personal question: 'What have you done in the last year which you are pleased with?'
- A few simple Maths sums.

Teaching tip

It is important not to ask students if they want to do the sheet. Rather put it in front of them and use a brisk cajoling attitude. Keep your voice and tone upbeat and enthusiastic to anticipate compliance.

Taking it further

An idea which helps this process along is to list students' names on the board and show that you are trying to prioritise their needs. You can then say: 'I'll be with you shortly Alice. Look, you're number five on my list!' This shows that they have been noticed and will be helped. It also teaches them a system of patience.

Behaviour management club

"Since going to the club I've realised that there's nothing wrong with me. We all face these behaviour challenges."

Here's a guide to forming a behaviour management club to help, advise and support each other on a regular basis.

Suggest starting up a weekly club to discuss and improve behaviour management across the school.

- Discuss frequently encountered behaviour problems and exchange techniques for dealing with them.
- Keep it friendly and upbeat and support each other.
- Keep it simple and straightforward: do not have minutes or paperwork or charts or statistics.

Over time you will find that the sharing of ideas removes that feeling of isolation so characteristic of teaching. You will realise that you are not the only one who is facing challenging behaviour. Focusing on behaviour management, acknowledging that it is one of your major concerns and regularly sharing your experiences with your colleagues will give you a sense of perspective on your own problems.

It will also provide a healthy balance away from the usual staffroom moans and groans which can so often make problems seem unsolvable. You will be putting your energy into finding solutions with like-minded people, rather than magnifying problems. Importantly, it will become a place where you know that you will be helped and supported by colleagues in a positive and useful way.

Sheer persistence

"I wanted to keep everyone happy but, by the end of the lesson, I found that my original lesson plan had not been completed at all."

Always be persistent about what you want to cover in your lesson.

The most effective strategy I know for dealing with challenging behaviour that attempts to distract you from your lesson plan is sheer persistence and resilience.

Good teachers know that they have to mould and adapt their plans in response to what actually happens in front of them. It helps if you can offer students choices about what they do in the lesson and how they should do it. But be careful, teachers can be too flexible. If you allow strong-minded students to argue about what they should be doing at every turn, they will eventually take over the class. If a teacher gives too much ground then it is doubly hard to impose authority next time.

The secret is to show some flexibility but to persist with your lesson and focus on what you want them to learn or achieve. When you are challenged about an important piece of work with comments like: 'Can we leave this bit? It's boring!' you must reply, with firm, quiet and determined persistence, that the piece of work is necessary and persuade them to do it. They will get used to the idea that the plan you have for your lesson is the plan that you follow, every single time.

It is tempting to bend and amend your plans in an attempt to appease vocal and disgruntled students, but you must remember that you are the manager of that class and you decide what is taught and how it is taught.

Teaching tip

Always have a 'trump card' as part of your persistent negotiation. You may, for example have in mind let's say, three areas of work: A, B and C. You could 'trade' work in area 'A' as long as 'B' and 'C' are completed. You could set out your worksheets using this strategy, with the core activities headed up: 'Important – must be completed by the end of the lesson', and the optional activities headed up 'optional'.

Invite in visitors

"Once I discovered what a rich resource it is to get people in presenting things, I've become more and more excited about the whole idea. So simple and yet so wonderful!"

Add variety, interest and dynamic to your lesson by inviting in as many people as you can to present in your class.

Often with a challenging class teachers feel, quite naturally, that it is too risky to bring in a visitor. However, a fantastic way to help a challenging class is to actively arrange for other people to come in and do a presentation. For example:

- Poets.
- Adventurers.
- Professionals talking about their jobs.
- Retired people reflecting on their lives.
- Experts on a particular subject.

There's something about the sense of occasion and the presence of the visitor in the room that really raises interest levels. Students always enjoy the surprise of someone new and you can be creative and inventive with the way you link the work you're doing to the visitor.

Very often people are flattered to be asked and will spend a great deal of time and effort preparing without expecting anything in return other than the experience of presenting. As you get more established in your school you can build up a network of contacts.

Preventing a fight

"Things were going OK for me as a new teacher. Then one day a nasty fight broke out in my classroom. The shock of it and the trouble it caused afterwards made me want to pack up and leave!"

The key to preventing a fight between students is to be vigilant so that the situation never escalates out of control.

Many teachers have experienced the horrific experience of a physical fight between two students in their classroom. When analysing the situation, almost always, if the teacher had intervened sooner, the fight would not have started.

Once a fight has started in your classroom you are in a catastrophic situation so you must develop a 'nose' for a particular type of behaviour between students which signals that there is trouble ahead, and you must always be on the lookout for it. Adopt a no-nonsense approach. If, for example, they ignore your requests to stop calling each other names then ask one of them to step outside the room and call for assistance.

With practise, you will differentiate between the type of banter normal for a particular group, and aggressive language and behaviour that, if left unchecked, could easily escalate into a fight. It is quite rare but when it happens it must be dealt with by early, brisk and firm intervention.

Teaching tip

If a fight is going to happen in a classroom it will most likely be right at the start, because you have had no control over the behaviour which has led to the state the students are in when they arrive at your door. Therefore you must be most alert, and use firm body language and a firm voice at the very opening of your lesson: show them that whatever happened before is not going to interrupt your lesson plan.

Taking it further

Ask other teachers what their experience has been in preventing fights in their classrooms and take very careful note of what they say.

Recovering from a disastrous lesson

"I had a nightmare lesson, and the next time I saw the class I hoped things would just magically sort themselves out. But they didn't, they got worse!"

If a lesson goes seriously wrong you must take assertive, carefully-planned action to put things right the next time you meet the class.

Sometimes a lesson will go so badly that the teacher feels that they have completely lost control and will understandably dread meeting the class again. You must deal with this situation in a systematic and logical way. The worse thing to do is to try to carry on as if nothing has happened. This is a situation where you must ask for help. Run through what you attempted to do and what went wrong with your head of department or other senior teacher.

Take firm action should be seen to be taken the very next lesson:

- Start the next lesson accompanied by a senior teacher.
- If necessary, ensure that the ringleaders have been isolated from the lesson.
- Announce to the class that you know the last lesson did not go well, that a lot of students ignored your instructions and that you want to return to good behaviour today. Let them know about any reprimands that have taken place since the last lesson, for example, ringleaders removed, detention letters sent and detentions given.
- Arrange for the senior teacher to return at the end for a report.

Help them get what they want

"When you start to see your students in terms of what they want to achieve, and then help them achieve it, it transforms the relationship."

How to help your students achieve their ambitions and, by doing so, encourage them to work more positively with you.

It is well known that building up a good strong teaching relationship with a challenging student is the key to success. But how exactly do you go about doing that?

As you chat with students, find out what it is that they really desire to achieve in life. Be patient, many students will claim that they have no particular interest in anything. However, gentle probing will reveal all kinds of clues. The main barrier is often their own lack of belief in their ability to achieve things. A teacher can never do better than when she helps a student achieve her ambitions.

Keep a notebook entitled 'My Students' Ambitions'. Have a page for each student and jot down notes about what they will need to know or what they will need to do to achieve their ambition. Also write down any obstacles they may face, and ways to overcome these.

Fill in each page with the students' help. I've found it works well if you ask them, very simply: 'I'd like to find out a few things about you and what you want to achieve in life, so that I can help you get there? Would that be OK?'

Bonus idea

Rather than have vague and general requirements try to work out a list of detailed things, from activities to take part in to books they should read, so that the student can start to work on achieving their goals straightaway and begin to feel they are on the road to success.

Low grade demotivation

"I got a 'G' in my mocks . I told you I was useless. Everyone else is getting 'Bs' and 'Cs'. What's the point?"

An unmotivated student with poor behaviour can become even more difficult to deal with when faced with low results. However, with careful reframing and an ability to look at the whole picture you can transform their attitude.

Teaching tip

Prepare a series of tests and assessments designed to pick up on things these students can succeed at. Credit can be given for things like attendance, attitude, helping others, problem solving and creative approach. This is a great way to improve confidence alongside the other work they are required to do.

With low-ability groups it is frequently the case that their results are very low in tests and mocks. The students, whose self-esteem will often already be low, will consider the low grades as proof that they are going to fail at everything. They question the point of further study and any lack of interest and poor behaviour that they have already shown may get even worse. The teacher's power to manage behaviour is weakened by this situation.

So what can a teacher do? A good way forward is to use reframing techniques which can transform the outcomes from negative to positive.

- Explain that although the grades are low now, the good news is that you have time to work together on this and you can still improve on them.
- Remind them that an employer would prefer to see some grade rather than none at all.
- Encourage them to think that from this moment onwards a positive mental attitude will provide a fresh new start, if they really want it. The grade is therefore no more than an early-warning sign to work harder.

Your trump card is to explain and emphasise that grades aren't everything, the most important thing is that they get a good reference from the school to a prospective employer, which should illustrate how well behaved they are, from now on, and how hard they try.

Tell them about past students whose grades may have been low but who nevertheless went on to achieve success. This sort of positive pep talk presented in a sincere way really does lift the spirits of the students.

Bonus idea ★

Keeping a collection of well-known people who are now rich, successful or famous but who had problems at school is also a powerful way to motivate students. You can make short presentations about them (see Idea 39 'Use using inspirational people to motivate students'). Emphasise to them that grades aren't everything. Qualities like good manners, how you stay calm under pressure, how kind you are, how well you get on with people, are all vital skills for future jobs and to succeed in life in general.

Taking it further

Keep a log of past students who have done well in their jobs and in their lives despite poor grades at school. Get permission from those students, of course, but then you can use the examples to encourage and inspire.

From time to time, when spirits are low, refer to the book and say things like: 'Come on, don't be down hearted! Don't you remember Ken, who got a 'G' in Science and is now the manager at XYZ Ltd? Who, in this room, am I going to be able to add to this book?'

You could take this idea further still and keep in touch with past students, making them 'friends of the school' and inviting them back to talk about how they have done. In this way the students get visions of what their own lives could become and it is a very powerful way to inspiring students with low grades.

Two-student dispute

"He doesn't ignore our problems. He tries to help us."

An ongoing dispute between students needs direct intervention from you.

Conflicts between students can be devastating to your lesson, not to mention the students' well-being. You can carry out a lot of superficial work in response like moving them to opposite sides of the classroom, isolating them and putting them on all sorts of reports. But if the problem continues, you need to do two things:

- Arrange a meeting with the two students.
- Listen to both sides of the problem.

Sometimes the problems are deeply entrenched and students just can't stand each other. You must explain to them that sometimes in life there are people who we don't get on with and that we all have to do things we don't like doing to get work done. Advise students to try to find common ground with other people so that they can establish areas of agreement. Encourage them to always remain calm, relaxed and cheerful; and to let little things go.

Then set them a challenge. 'If you two can work together in my next lesson without trouble I will be delighted with you both because I know how hard it is. I'm not expecting you to become best friends. All I want you to do is tolerate each other peacefully. Do you think you could do that difficult thing for me?'

By showing a direct interest and understanding of the problem and by setting them a specific challenge you will see an improvement in the next lesson.

Taking it further

Another technique I have tried is to get the students to write out, in detail, how they feel and why. Then I ask them to suggest ways in which the situation can be improved. The important thing is to then have a meeting with the two students present and another member of staff (this is essential). The viewpoints, from both sides are read out by the teacher and the focus is then on the question: 'How can we improve this?' It is amazing how the two of them then often come up with suggestions which might help. There is no way that you could gain that sort of insight into their problems without their input. Your role could then be to oversee how the improvements might work in practice.

Reaching a compromise

"There is no denying it, she is a fair teacher."

This idea encourages cooperation because students see you applying the rules in a fair way.

If you consider yourself to be a strict teacher – who never lets anything go and follows the rules to the letter – then I've got news for you. You will stress yourself out, be unpopular and you will not see good behaviour in your classes.

If, on the other hand, you let students off far too easily and do not consistently apply the rules and think that being a 'nice guy' is enough, then you will find that your authority will be undermined and the students will do as they please in your classes.

All teachers need to achieve an intelligent compromise. Let's look at an example. Rachel arrives at your lesson, eating a sandwich. A strict teacher would demand that the food is put away straight away. After all, that's the rule isn't it? A soft teacher might let her carry on eating it at her desk. But for a situation like this, and countless others, you need to reach a compromise. You could say something like 'Rachel, you know it's against the rules to eat in lesson. If I let you do it then everyone will want to do it and my classroom will look like a canteen. OK, OK, you had no breakfast today. Fine. You can stand outside and eat half of it. Then wrap up what's left, put it in your bag and back to the class. But Rachel, please don't do this again. Thanks.' Smile and keep the conversation brisk. Problem solved, without conflict.

Teaching tip

With situations like this it is vital to explain why breaking the rule is a problem. Then show understanding of their particular situation and offer a suggested compromise solution pointing out that you would like to see improvements next time.

Rounding up the lesson

"I hate the ends of lessons. The students get restless, pack up, leave their seats and try to leave before I've finished. What can I do?"

The best way to end a lesson is to focus on the next one.

Towards the end of your lesson, before the students put away their books, display a PowerPoint presentation with the following headings:

- Next lesson we are going to...
- This is what I want you to do to prepare...

It is important to keep it brief, clear and simple. Ask students to think about how you are going to prepare the work you are setting. Doing this has the following results:

- It gives a focused purpose to the time at the end of the present lesson.
- It will hold students attention until you are ready to let them go.
- It sends a strong signal about your own organisational abilities, showing the definite direction and purpose of your teaching.
- It also makes the start of the next lesson smoother.

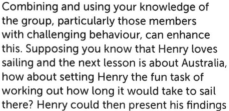

Wait it out

"I tried to shout down the noise but they were in a frenzy and my shouting made it worse."

If the class arrive in a heightened state of excitement you must give time and space for the energy to settle.

Supposing that just prior to your lesson there has been a fire drill, or a fight, or one of many reasons that can lead to a highly excitable group entering your room. You allow the normal settling down time but unfortunately find that a significant number of the class just will not settle. This can be very disturbing for a teacher and the natural reaction is to act strongly here. The problem is that your annoyance will feed into the whirlpool of unsettled energy and make it worse.

Rather than get annoyed, the idea here is to do the exact opposite. Stay calm and stand still. Say nothing. Silently adopt a strong, calm body posture in a prominent part of the room and have a facial expression of firm, calm, overseeing disapproval. Wait patiently. Do not say or do anything. The students will know that they have pushed you too far and there is a certain power in your stillness and calmness.

This waiting allows the energy in the room to drain away a little. The students are not quite sure what you are going to do next. Wait and wait longer, knowing that the energy is settling. Only when the group has calmed, say in a quiet, calm and firm voice: 'I have waited ten minutes (or however long) for you to settle. I have spent a lot of time preparing your lesson today. I realise that something has unsettled you but enough is enough. We need to start our work now.' Then start your lesson.

Teaching tip

If, after a reasonable amount of time has passed, the class remains out of control, then you must call for support. Don't just carry on with your lesson regardless; a lesson that starts off on a bad footing like this will not run smoothly.

Taking it further

If you are aware beforehand that a class are going to be particularly unsettled (perhaps the lesson will follow an exciting assembly or a wet lunch break), then stop them before they enter your room and let them in two at a time, handing them a simple worksheet for them to immediately start work on.

65

Hit the slow motion button

"I regret what I said to him but I was angry and every teacher has their limits."

Have a 'slow motion button', allowing you thinking time in the heat of the situation.

Imagine this scenario. You ask a student why he or she is doing no work and messing about and he or she rips up the worksheets, throws them on the floor and says: 'You're a useless teacher and this work is stupid and boring!' You have been up late the night before preparing the worksheet and are reaching the end of your patience with this aggressive student and reactively say: 'Well you're a useless student if you tear up my work like that! How dare you!' The student then pushes the chair at you, injuring your leg, and runs out of the room saying: 'I'm going to get my dad on you for calling me useless!'

High-stress situations can suddenly develop rapidly, particularly with challenging students. Your instinctive reaction, although natural, can contribute to the problems and add fuel to the fire. So when the heat is on, have a 'slow motion button' in your mind. Picture what it looks like. Maybe it is bright yellow and when you press it soft music starts gently playing. When you push this button, you deliberately slow everything down allowing you crucial thinking time to consider your response.

When you get into the habit of using this technique then you will find that provocative behaviour actually triggers the slow motion response. This will give you a vital few moments of thought time to restore your control. It will save you from reacting rashly and may even save your job.

The root of the problem

"I like my teacher because somehow he knew there was a problem. He actually cares."

A lot of behaviour problems are recurrent and sometimes you need to get to the root of them to gain any ground.

It is surprising how much disruption in a classroom is of a recurrent type. Busy teachers are often so occupied dealing with what's in front of them that they don't have the time to step back and analyse the situation.

It is a wise use of time to step back a little and try to see what the underlying causes may be. Here are some common examples:

- Late to lessons. Is there a pattern? Maybe it is always an afternoon lesson because the student goes home for lunch.
- After break do certain students disrupt because they've been playing football, forget to get a drink and arrive thirsty and uncomfortable to your lesson?
- Does one student behave very strangely because during break they were bullied and had nowhere to go?

The key thing here is to keep good, clear, accurate notes to help you identify 'hotspot' areas. Share your information with other teachers to see if patterns emerge.

The next step is to approach the student and say something like: 'Ellie, I've noticed that after break you don't seem to want to do much work and you seem worried. Normally you're such a good student. Is there anything the school can do to help?' Avoid sounding confrontational and make it clear that you want to help.

Teaching tip

Be clear that the offer of help is from the 'school' because the student may prefer to discuss the matter with another teacher. Be patient and give the student the opportunity to think about it and come back to you later. Don't forget to ask again in a future lesson if they don't come back to you.

Hidden bad behaviour

"He wasn't doing any of the work I set him, but for most of the time he stayed quiet and I didn't have time to make him do the task."

Some students get away with doing next to nothing every lesson and this idea helps correct that.

Some students do not appear badly behaved. Far from it, they are often friendly, polite and cooperative, and they are never rude or argumentative. However, they don't actually complete any work in your lesson.

There is a huge temptation when dealing with a challenging group to let these students get on with it but they must be dealt with. If you don't, three serious problems will emerge:

- The students will get so used to doing no work that it will become increasingly difficult to get them to do anything at all.
- It will give other students a great excuse not to work either. All they have to say is 'He's not working so why should I?'
- The less students actually focus on work the more likely they are to disrupt the lesson.

Once you've identified this group of students try the following strategies:

- Make them aware that you are monitoring their work.
- Set small step-by-step targets for them to reach.
- Keep reminding them of the purpose and reason for the work – it is to help them.
- Praise any improvement you see and encourage them along.

You will find students will eventually start to work more and they will be less likely to disrupt your lesson.

Dealing with calling out

"I used to stop what I was saying and wait for quiet. I found that I had to wait a long time and it became very tedious and tiring and harder to restart."

A technique to effectively deal with students who call out.

One of the most common and disruptive things a teacher has to deal with is students calling out when they are trying to speak to the whole class.

If you stop what you're saying and tell the student off in a harsh way it changes the mood of the class, the momentum is lost and it invites further calling out in the 'space' which emerges. The best way to deal with this is to keep your delivery at a fairly brisk pace and respond to the calling out as explained below, rather than stopping the whole flow and showing annoyance.

Try to discourage others from joining in and calling out by saying: 'Excuse me, class, for a moment,' then give a powerful open hand signal to the whole class (which indicates that you will return your attention to them in a moment) and say to the student who called out: 'It's great that you've got some ideas and I do want to hear them. But please let me speak to the class as a whole first.' If the student calls out again, repeat the process but slightly more firmly, but still keep the focus on the forward pace of the lesson.

It might help to increase the speed of your delivery, forcing the class to listen more attentively. There are times when it is appropriate to stop in mid-sentence and glare at the interrupter, but really try to keep that pace going and deflect the interrupters with swift appropriate comments.

Teaching tip

You don't have to speak to the whole class at the start of the lesson. Sometimes it is better to get them working on the starter and then, when the time is right, speak to the class as a whole. Also, keep it short, snappy and to the point.

Knowing what to ignore

"He's getting on my nerves. He picks on every little thing. You can't do anything!"

One of the key skills in teaching is knowing when to ignore poor behaviour and when to react to it. This idea will save you a lot of unnecessary energy.

A good teacher wants a forward-moving flow in their lessons with minimum or no confrontation. If you react to every little interruption or piece of bad behviour in a lesson your effectiveness will be diminished when you need to reprimand something really important. It is far better to let little things go, employing a kind of strategic blind eye, and broadcast pleasant and positive comments instead. Then, when something is important the class will sit up and take note of you.

Be clear in your head which behaviours you are going to pick up on and which you will leave be. If someone has made a mistake and is crossing it out a little too energetically, let it be. If someone's making unkind comments to another student and this continues, then it's time to step in. Give a brief reason as to why you have requested a change in behaviour from someone. For example: 'Lottie, if you make those unkind comments, Jack will get upset. They have to stop now.'

Taking it further

Take the time and trouble to visit other classes by arrangement and make notes on the sorts of things that teachers reprimand for, and the sorts of things they ignore and this will help you in your own development. You will see patterns of behaviour and categories of seriousness. Discuss with the experienced teachers why they reprimand some things and why they let other things slide and you will learn great lessons indeed.

Stay in control

"The teacher is so wrapped up helping individual students that the class goes crazy and she doesn't even notice it."

One of the most important but necessary skills of a teacher is to be able to help an individual while at the same time keeping a close eye on the whole class.

It is very frustrating when a teacher is trying to help an individual student and finds that the noise levels and disruption of the class gets out of hand as soon as her attention is off of the whole class.

I have noticed that there are teachers who carry on regardless, helping individuals and letting the class get out of control. There are also those teachers who simply never help individuals, telling them to 'wait until the class settles'. So how do you manage this situation successfully?

A good idea is to have a procedure where you call up the student to your desk, get him to stand to one side so that you can review his work and at the same time watch the class. The comments you then make can be on two levels: one where you comment about the work to the individual and then the 'broadcast comments' to the group as a whole, like 'Come on Alfie, that's enough...' or 'Jess, I hope you're asking Susan a question about the work I set. I'll be over to see how you're doing in a moment.' The reason that this simple idea works so well is that the whole class hears the comments, realise that they remain under your watchful gaze and won't misbehave.

Teaching tip

You don't have to just call the student to your desk. You can go to them or you can call them to the back of the room if you are standing there observing the class anyway. The important thing is to keep the two levels of comments going throughout the class.

Put on a show!

"Teaching is 80% theatre and 20% content."

One of the most common problems facing teachers is the number of students who simply don't pay attention and the considerable chain reaction of disruption that this causes. Use this technique to bring your content to life.

For many students it seems that the lesson is something that they have to just suffer. They become involved in a lot of low-level disruption to amuse themselves and ward off the boredom.

There is no magic trick to make students pay attention. However, I have found that there is one thing that is effective at getting and keeping students' attention. Many teachers talk in the abstract about their subject matter, referring to non-specific things or vague concepts. It is very hard for the mind to be stimulated without details and facts. So try to be specific in what you say. Try to make details vivid, dramatic and full of action to stimulate your class's imagination.

For example, you might be teaching Newton's theory of gravity. You could present it in a dull, flat, factual way or you could get them to picture in their minds a huge, bright green apple, with a little worm in it, falling out of the tree and thumping Newton on the head. Describe the bruise. Do a dramatic representation of him gazing up at the tree, rubbing his head.

By stimulating the students' imagination you can bring any subject to life. Eventually it will become more interesting for them to listen to you than to mess about.

No arguing!

"I was simply trying to point out why she should not behave like that and I ended up arguing with the whole class. I felt devastated by the experience."

This idea gives powerful ways to avoid an argument.

Under no circumstances must you allow yourself to be drawn into an argument with a student in the classroom. Arguing is time consuming, stressful and creates an atmosphere of confrontation, something you should always be working to avoid.

An argument provides a platform for the students to openly challenge your authority. So if a student attempts to drag you into an argument, deploy the following strategies:

- Stop the student and tell them that you'll discuss the issue at the end of the lesson. Immediately return your focus to the work in hand.
- If the student persists (and they often do), calmly repeat that you will not argue with them.
- Always use a firm, business-like voice in situations like this.
- If the student still tries to involve you in an argument you must explain that you have repeatedly asked them to stop and you will have no choice but to ask them to leave the class if they continue. Follow through with the threat if necessary.

Teaching tip

Some students may have a valid grievance and perhaps do not intend to disrupt the class by trying to argue with you. In that case, talk to them after the class – making sure that one other adult is present – and take the opportunity to calmly sit down and work out a solution.

Taking it further

If some students are in the habit of trying to start arguments to disrupt classes then it is important to arrange a meeting with them in the presence of a senior teacher. Present them with the fact that they have on many occasions deliberately tried to disrupt lessons by insisting on an argument. Once they are confronted and warned about the consequences of their actions you are a long way into solving the problem.

Stop bullying in its tracks

"I want to leave this job. I've had parents shouting at me saying I can't control the class and that their son has been bullied in my lesson. I didn't even know!"

Watching out for the early signs of bullying and then acting on it decisively and promptly will save everyone a great deal of pain and anguish.

Teaching tip

It can be hard to spot the signs of bullying. If you make it an absolute rule that there are to be no unkind comments made between students, then enforcing that rule will solve most of the potential trouble flashpoints. At the most basic level if two or more students direct unkind comments at one particular student, particularly if it is repeated, then take that as the hallmark that trouble is in store.

Look out for students, particularly if there are two (or more) against one, making unkind comments to another. Warn them to stop and if they ignore you or try to deflect it by saying 'We're only joking, we're having a laugh, he calls us names too' then you must act immediately.

If the comments continue, call for support from another member of staff and insist that the culprits are taken to a discipline support room (or the appropriate place provided by your school). Involve the necessary staff and make sure that the situation is investigated and resolved before you allow the students back into your class for future lessons.

It is also vital to explain your actions to the rest of the class. For example, 'If this behaviour (don't say 'bullying' it causes an unhelpful argument) continues despite my warnings then I will have everyone involved isolated from this lesson right away. I simply will not have this kind of behaviour!' Do not get involved in discussing with them the details of what you mean by 'this kind of behaviour' – they know exactly what you mean.

Failure to spot the prelude to bullying and then failure to act, or as I have witnessed many times, failure to promptly remove those involved will almost certainly lead to devastating consequences.

Bonus idea ⭐

In my experience, tackling bullies is one of the most challenging parts of the job. When bullies are confronted they are very expert at trying to turn around the situation to make it seem that they are the victims and they will give plentiful examples of terrible things that have been directed at them. They will then use their trump card and direct their anger at you and accuse you of taking sides. This is why it is vital to never tackle a bully on your own. Always have another adult with you and whatever the student says or does, always direct the focus calmly back to the behaviour you saw that was unacceptable.

Taking it further

It is a great idea to gather 'intelligence' from pastoral heads about who is bullying who so that you can plan ahead. If you know that students in your class are involved in bullying, meet them at the door and say to them: 'I realise that you've had one or two issues lately with Zak so I want you to know that I'm looking forward to sending a great report to your head of year at the end of this lesson to show that you've moved on and are getting on with some good work.' Say it with an upbeat attitude, show them a blank report clearly headed 'Positive Report' and make sure that at the end of the lesson you do send it and tell them you've sent it. This pre-empting of trouble often completely stops anything going wrong in its tracks. The students quickly realise that you're on to them and that you're watching everything.

Moving stubborn students

"I asked her to move seats and she point blank refused! What can I do? I can't pick her up and carry her to the other chair!"

It is not easy to move a reluctant student to a different seat but this idea will help.

Moving students can be a problem. If the student refuses and your authority takes a body blow in front of the whole class. You should have a seating plan already in place to minimise the risk of needing to move a student. If however, you do need to move someone and they refuse, what should you do?

After a number of warnings have been given, walk over to the seat you want the student to move to and pull it away from the desk. Then calmly and confidently walk back to the student, stand at a distance of about half a metre from him or her and holding one open hand towards him or her and the other hand pointing to the destination seat say: 'Right, move to that seat please.' It is important now to wait and hold that pose. The student will probably argue and say things like: 'I'm not moving. Why should I?' Stay calm and repeat your instructions. Do not raise your voice. Say: 'I need to get on with teaching my class. I'm waiting.' Then continue to wait. After a while say: 'Move over there please.'

There is a strong psychological pressure brought to bear in this situation. It is surprising how even the most reluctant student will begin to move at this point. Ignore any comments that they may mumble as they start to collect up their stuff (this is to be expected). As soon as they have moved make no further comment but get back to teaching your lesson.

In the rare cases when the student still won't move, you must make a point of saying: 'OK, I will see you at the end of the lesson about this.' Continue teaching but ensure that:

- There is a meeting at the end of the lesson with you, the student and the head of department to discuss this (if the head of department is not available, book a meeting as soon as possible).
- Make sure that a sanction is given and a letter is sent home reporting the incident.
- Make absolutely certain that the class see the student working in the new seat next lesson. This may take a senior member of staff to be present but it must be done. If not, your authority will have been breached in front of the whole class and they will see that she got away with it.
- Remember, you don't have to solve everything on the spot, the important thing is the class sees that you are in control.

The reason you need to move a student is due to that person causing trouble in that place in the room. Rather than suddenly moving them it is sensible to step up the 'temperature' of the warnings, before you move them, in this way:

- First warning: 'Michelle, it's not working where you're sitting. Settle down quickly please or we will have to do something about it, won't we?'
- Second warning: 'Michelle, I've asked you several times now to settle down. You are ignoring my requests. If you carry on like that we shall move you to this seat over here.'
- Third warning: 'OK Michelle, you've had your final warnings, get your stuff and move over to this seat please.'

Taking it further

In an extreme case, where there may be a threat of harm to other students, and a student refuses to move, or indeed, refuses to leave the classroom, then it may be better to move the whole class out to another room.

Behaviour bargaining

"I like my teacher. What we agreed was fair."

Many students work better when they feel that they have negotiated a 'deal' rather than having something imposed on them where they have no control.

The central task of any teacher is to get the students working in a way that will help them to learn, because students who are engaged in their work don't have time to act up or mess about. However, some students will only want to do enough to 'get by' (leaving them time to disrupt the class). But by bargaining with them you can get them to work to small goals and achieve results. If carefully used, the students will feel that they have gained a comparative advantage over what was previously expected and will be more likely to cooperate with you.

Here are some examples:

- If a student has stopped working and says the task is 'boring' try saying: 'I tell you what we could do. You've worked hard up until now so how about just doing three more questions and we can do the rest tomorrow?'
- If a student repeatedly gets out of his seat, try saying: 'Look Gavin, you mustn't be out of your seat. You know that. But I can also see that you get agitated and have to stretch your legs now and again. Let's try this: stay in your seat until eleven o'clock and then have a very short walk around. But then you must agree to get back to work. Is that fair?'

A letter of praise

"A lot of teachers say they'll send a good letter home but they never do. This teacher gives you the letter there and then and you can bring it home straight away."

Supplying limited but immediate rewards is very effective as part of your overall behaviour management strategy.

Have a supply of letters typed out on headed paper with a space for the student's name and the specific reason for praise for you to fill in. The great thing with this idea is that the letter can be given to them at the end of the lesson and students get used to this immediacy, which makes the reward effective.

Remind them of the letters at the start of the lesson by announcing: 'Now don't forget everyone, I have three letters to hand out at the end for good work. I'm going to be looking for good things all through the lesson. Remember, if you do your best today it could be you!'

This puts the challenge in their minds at the start of the lesson. It is a good idea to limit the letters to three. Handing out countless letters will devalue them and take away the effectiveness of the idea.

Remember, like so many ideas with behaviour management techniques, it is how you prepare the ground and present ideas to your class that is key to its success.

Teaching tip

Sometimes, when this idea is really successful many students may expect a letter and are very unhappy when they don't get one. I have found that to manage this you need to do two things:

1   Make sure that you announce the names of the students to get letters at the end of the lesson. This will avoid disruption and arguments during the lesson about why some students didn't get them.

2   Tell students whose behaviour and work certainly did warrant a letter, but who just weren't in the top three on the day, that you will write their names in your rewards book and send the letters in the next few days.

Separate the behaviour from the student

"I think my teacher is fair. I was out of order but I think he does care and he still likes me."

You will be respected and successful in the long run if you separate the behaviour from the student. The two can be dealt with separately. This idea is the next logical step from Idea 49 'Telling them off with praise.'

Teaching tip

You may think that the 'blueprint' for telling off students is to shout, get angry and attempt to come over as the kind of teacher who must not be crossed. But it is so much more effective if you don't 'attack' them (which is what it can seem like from their point of view), try to reprimand only their behaviour and even make them feel good about the situation. You must be clear and fair, reason with them and by using this technique of separating person from behaviour your success in controlling desirable outcomes will be transformed.

As a teacher you must remember that students' feelings work exactly like yours. Anyone who is criticised will naturally get defensive and it is the same for students. Therefore, if you focus the criticism onto the *behaviour* rather than the person, you will get a far better outcome.

A good way to ensure that you only criticise the bad behaviour is to take care with the language you use. For example, supposing Eleanor keeps interrupting you but is not responding to the normal techniques. Say: 'Eleanor, I have asked you several times to settle down but you seem to be intent on ignoring me. You know that the rule for not calling out is so that everyone has a chance to listen and contribute. I have no choice but to keep you back for ten minutes. The rules are for all of us. I know you can really succeed in this subject but we have to deal with this matter before we can get back to our good work again.'

The mobile phone

"I told him to put his phone away and he ignored me. I threatened all sorts of sanctions and I got quite annoyed. Two minutes later he was texting on it again. What do I do?"

This idea gives a clear strategy for how to cope with the single most annoying problem that teachers deal with today – the mobile phone.

Most schools have very strict policies regarding mobile phones. Unfortunately, these policies are not always enforced.

The fact that mobiles can take photos and videos and then these can be put online makes taking a mobile out in a lesson a very serious offence. I really think that there should be zero-tolerance. Emphasise to your students that you will not allow mobiles to be used in your lesson for any reason. Ensure that senior colleagues also enforce the rule. Make it absolutely clear that you will not tolerate them.

If a student does produce a mobile then explain to them that if they don't put it away you will lock it in a secure cupboard or drawer, show them the key. The headteacher will then give it to their parents after school. Nine times out of ten the student will put it away. Warn them that if it reappears a senior teacher will be called immediately.

Arrange with your colleagues to make the procedure for retrieving confiscated mobiles as difficult as possible for students. Insist that the parents must come to the school to collect it. The student will not want to be deprived of his mobile or involve their parents.

Teaching tip

Students who challenge your authority by frequently getting out their mobile phone must be dealt with differently. Warn the student that because he frequently ignores the rules his mobile will be confiscated for next lesson, even before he enters the room. Once you have identified such students, arrange to have a senior member of staff meet you and the student at the door at the beginning of the next lesson and ask him to hand over his mobile before enters your room.

Reflect and learn

"When I started teaching I thought I would pick it up quite quickly. Then I began to realise that teaching is a craft of immense skill. The good news, I found, is that you can learn it."

Actively seek ways to improve by watching the experts and adapting their methods.

There are two pathways for tackling behaviour management. You can struggle along, just keep repeating what you do lesson after lesson. Your job will be a constant battle and your principal role will be 'damage limitation'. This type of teacher is so caught up 'in' his job that he can't step back and look 'at' it to work out how to improve.

The other way is so much better. At every opportunity, ask yourself 'How could I have done that better?' It is as simple as that.

You should consider:

- When something goes wrong how could you have handled it in a different way?
- Regularly consult with other teachers about their techniques.
- Read everything about the subject of behaviour management; go on courses and watch training videos.
- Experiment with different techniques.
- Be creative in your approach.

If you persevere with this idea the following rewards will be seen:

- You will feel happier, more in control and less tired.
- Your students will enjoy your lessons more.
- Your colleagues will respect you.
- The parents will admire you.

'I haven't got a pen'

"Lots of my students never bring a pen. I've tried detention but a parent complained. I've tried giving them out but it's costing me a lot to keep the box replenished as I never seem to get them back!"

This idea shows a procedure that can be easily put into place to help solve a very annoying and common problem.

Students proclaiming they do not have a pen is a common problem and can be very irritating. If you freely give out pens you will find that the students have no incentive to remember to bring one. On the other hand, not providing a spare pen can result in the student using it as an excuse not to work. It can also lead to an argument right at the point of the lesson when you seek to get the momentum going. So what should you do?

A great idea is to have some spare pens ready *but*:

- Make sure that each pen has bright sticky tape on it, use a variety of colours.
- Make a point of saying that you will need a word with the student about this at the end of the lesson (this causes the student inconvenience).
- Write the name of the student on the board with the colour of the pen which has been lent out.

The advantages of this is that it allows the lesson to flow, but makes a point that there are consequences for the student as they must talk to you after class (otherwise they will never remember to bring a pen) and the simple name-on-the-board/colour system ensures you get your pen back.

Teaching tip

You could also lend pens in only one colour, say green ink. Then, when you review the student's exercise book over a series of lessons you can see how often he forgets his pen. This is useful when you're discussing with him how to solve the problem.

Presentation club

"I didn't know that my PE teacher loved science fiction books so much. I love science fiction too and now we chat about it a lot."

By arranging for teachers and other staff to share their passions and interests with the students the general community feel of the school improves and with it the behaviour of the students.

Every teacher has a passion for something other than school work. Why not take a bit of time to harness this rich resource for the benefit of teachers and students by forming a 'Presentation Club' where each teacher prepares a presentation based on their particular passion or expert knowledge.

This idea has very significant advantages:

- It is highly enjoyable; teachers love to demonstrate their passions and interests in the right environment and context.
- Teachers will be seen in a new light by students and will seem more approachable.
- The students' learning is enhanced by listening to teachers they wouldn't normally meet.
- Behaviour improves dramatically because it captures the students' imaginations.
- It brings to the fore the sense that the school is a community, not a set of separate years and classes.
- It engenders teamwork between colleagues.
- It allows you to observe other teachers at their best and enables you to adopt their techniques into your own teaching and presentation skills.
- It opens up new lines of communication with students as they see who else shares their own interests.

Teaching tip

Be sure to extend the club as widely as you can. Across departments, across year groups and across ability groups. The idea is to uncover hidden interests that students and staff members have in common. Stay away from the core curriculum to really see students' and teachers' true passions shine.

Taking it further

If the project is successful, invite other members of staff to join in including dinner ladies, caretakers, lab technicians and even governors and parents. Eventually everyone will want to join in and contribute.

'I'm not feeling well'

"If I let them go to the nurse too easily they see me as a soft touch. If I don't let them go and they are really unwell could I get in trouble? I'm not a nurse, I'm a teacher. How do I know?"

This idea outlines a simple and effective strategy for knowing what to do when someone is unwell.

It is challenging to deal with a student who claims to not be well but is just making it up as a reason not to work. It may be genuine, of course. Your job is to use professional judgement to decide what to do. If a student requests to go to the nurse say: 'Look Sophie, just try and get on with your work quietly for ten minutes and if you still feel unwell then we'll see what we can do. If you feel worse before then let me know straight away.' Keep an eye on the student. Is she acting as if she's unwell or furtively messing about with her friends?

In most cases the student will get on with her work and forget that she was unwell. If after ten minutes she is still complaining then send her to the nurse. Also, don't ask her after ten minutes, see if she remembers to ask you.

In other cases you will be confronted by a more difficult situation where a student is not working, claims to be unwell and yet will not go to the nurse. In this case, give them a reasonable amount of time to sit quietly and then offer them the choice of either getting on with their work or going to the nurse. It is important that there is no middle ground here. You are showing the whole class that you care but that there is a procedure in place.

Teaching tip

For a student who is always asking to go to the nurse check, by consultation with the nurse, to see if there is an underlying issue to this and then seek advice from senior staff about what to do.

Role play training

"The fight in my room caused me so much upset that I'm seriously thinking of leaving the teaching profession."

Use this role play training activity with colleagues to explore high tension scenarios and work out the best way to deal with them.

Mini Role Play Script

Characters: A= Teacher; B= Isaac (student); C= Sean (student).

B If he said that then tell him to get stuffed!

C You tell him and he'll knock you out mate! (*body language indicates rising aggression*)

B I'll get my uncle down here and he'll have the lot of you! (*rising aggression*)

A Right! That's enough of all that. Let's get on with the Shakespeare, please. (*firm voice but also very wary*)

C (*totally ignoring the teacher*) Is that the uncle that Tracy knocked out last week? (*mocking voice, starts to rise from seat... pre-fight ritual body language sequence begins*) He's an idiot mate!

A I've said that's enough. Now settle down! (*shouts and tries to be firm and controlling but teacher's behaviour has no effect on the escalation of aggression*)

B (*anger now directed at teacher, who is in the way*) I ain't settling nothing! He's gonna get it (*starts moving towards his opponent and the whole class fall silent in anticipation of a fight*)

A (*trying to hide panic*) Amy, could you go to reception and get a senior teacher quickly please? Quickly!

Run though the role play a few times, experiment to discover how the dynamics of tension change. By doing this you will see and feel what the best way to respond is.

Afterwards, discuss the following points:

- At what point should the teacher intervene?
- Why is it so important to have a prearranged contingency plan for getting help quickly to the class?
- What is the most appropriate body language and tone of voice a teacher should use in such a scenario?
- What should the teacher do as the students face up to each other?
- If a fight breaks out what action should the teacher take? (This is a vital point and I have found there to be much misunderstanding and vagueness about it. What are the school's procedures?)
- Should the teacher be offered support afterwards?

The idea of the role play is to experiment and discover. In practice, of course, it is better to avoid letting the situation develop in the first place. But how do you do that? Make sure that as the students enter your room you can stand in a strategic position by the door and 'sniff out' signs of trouble as they enter. It is there and then that you could direct one of them to wait outside the room while a senior member of staff is called. This is before tensions rise. There are clear warning signs to look out for and spotting them early and acting on them is a vital skill for a teacher to have.

> **Bonus idea** ★
>
> It is a good idea to get together with experienced colleagues and make a list of the signs that indicate that trouble is to follow. You won't spot them all, of course, but using certain strategies will lower the risk of a fight happening on your watch.

Call for help

"The class descended into chaos, students were hurt and property got damaged. I shouldn't have let it get that bad. I should have called for help."

If your normal professional techniques fail, call for help.

Imagine the following situation. You begin your lesson in the normal way but maybe the class is a little less settled than normal. Something is not quite right. Rosie decides to run to the front and make a big drama about putting something in the bin. Chloe bursts out with uncontrolled laughter. Ethan starts thumping his partner in the arm and so on. You use your usual techniques to gain control but they fail. Disruption is spreading and you are rapidly losing control of the situation. The odds are stacked up against you because it's 30 to one.

There is really only one thing you must do in this situation: call in the cavalry (a member of the senior management team). There are those teachers who think that calling for help is an admittance of failure and a sign of weakness, but this is not the case. In fact, it is a strength.

To continue trying to battle against the class described above is not only an error of judgement but is also very dangerous because it could quickly deteriorate into anarchy and physical harm. To not call for help in such a situation is an abuse of the trust parents place in teachers as professional guardians of their children.

Thankfully, it is quite rare to need to call for help but when the situation warrants it, do not hesitate.

Abuse outside school

"I was shopping in the supermarket and a group of students shouted abuse at me. I confronted them and the abuse got far worse. When I got home I was so upset I wanted to resign."

Abusive comments from students outside school is a serious matter and you should not attempt to deal with it alone.

If a student makes an abusive comment to you in the street, tempting though it may be, never attempt to deal with it there and then. To stop the situation getting out of control, take it up with senior staff next time you are at the school. Arrange a meeting with the head or another senior teacher, the student and his parents or guardians. It must be made clear that the matter is very serious. A school's ethos about polite behaviour extends outside the school as well. It must be made clear that further abusive comments in the street will not be tolerated under any circumstances.

Make sure the incident is officially recorded by the school and keep a record of it yourself. It is best to end the meeting with a tone of forgiveness and reconciliation. Treat the student as you normally would in school and certainly make no further reference to the incident.

If, in rare cases, the abusive behaviour continues in the street rely on the school's policy. Never try to deal with it as an individual.

Teaching tip

If you are subjected to abusive comments in the street from your students, your natural reaction is to get angry and react in some way. The thing to remember is that teaching young people requires an extraordinary capacity for patience and self-control. Always stay calm and think carefully before you act. Remove yourself from the situation as soon as you can and rely on the system in place at your school to deal with it for you. Remember that the students are not abusing you personally. They are abusing you as an authority figure and one of your main items of 'armour', always, is self-control and reacting calmly.

Better than a detention

"I seem to spend half my time writing out detention letters and the other half chasing them up because students haven't turned up."

This idea will save you time and improve behaviour.

Teachers frequently resort to issuing detentions. It seems straightforward but there are major drawbacks involved:

- It can create resentment and actually make the situation worse.
- You become involved in a world of form filling that takes up your precious time.
- You are burdened by having to check that the student actually attends the detention.
- If they don't attend, you have to go through the whole process again.
- Detentions are one of the biggest causes of disagreements with parents.

Teachers have very few sanctions at their disposal and as a last resort detentions can be very useful. There is, however, a better way to deal with things. Try using a formal detention warning letter, sent home to parents, to resolve the matter first.

By issuing a warning letter instead of an actual detention, you will find that, after initial protests, the student's behaviour will improve and they will be anxious to check with you that their behaviour is seen by you as being better by the end of the lesson.

This idea works because it involves minimal work compared to the work involved with a detention and at the same time produces better behaviour.

The court jester

"I suppose I do like to be the centre of attention really. I get thrown out of most classes but with her I can mess about a bit but I stay in the class and sort of get on with it. She sort of understands me."

How to micro-manage a student who is always centre of attention.

Some students are experts at commanding attention using a wide range of techniques. They act as a sort of 'court jester' to the class. They pride themselves on misbehaviour and far from being worried by reprimands they actually thrive on them.

I have found that confronting this type of behaviour head-on is not the best way. I remember a 'no nonsense' teacher whose strict approach resulted in the student being moved to another group permanently. It solved the problem for that teacher but what about the next teacher who received the student?

I have developed a two-tier system. You continue to manage your class with the tried and tested techniques but within that you manage the challenging student on another level.

You must micro-manage him, keep a closer eye on him and give instant feedback when he crosses the line. It is a close-monitoring process and your comments must be fair, firm and frequent. In effect, you are allowing him space to act out a little bit, but at the same time managing his behaviour neatly within the context of the whole class. Make most of the comments close up to the student and use this type of approach: 'Well done Thomas, you're doing well with that work. Just bring the noise level down a little, yes?'

Teaching tip

To enhance this approach carefully set up lots of situations where the class are ready to do a fun activity but say: 'We cannot start until we are all sitting quietly.' and look across to the court jester. You will find that the power and persuasion of the whole class, together with your patient approach, will help manage his behaviour.

Don't up the stakes too quickly

"I have written out several detention slips, I've shouted and ordered people out of the room but the class is still playing up. What should I do now?"

Don't escalate the consequences too quickly or you'll have nothing left to work with.

One of the most common problems for teachers is the use of too many sanctions too soon. The teacher 'ups the stakes' and issues sanction after sanction but when faced with a class whose behaviour deteriorates further, is left with no sanctions to use.

Slowing down your use of reprimands works extremely well. For example, instead of moving a student who misbehaves, first try saying to them: 'If this poor behaviour continues I'm going to have to consider moving you to another seat.' Notice that initially you are warning that you will 'consider' moving him. This technique allows you more space and more time to think and it allows the student more time to think about the consequences of their actions. If they continue to misbehave you can warn them that they *will* be moved the next time and if they persist, finally move them.

This technique allows you to control the class by using a verbal warning so the tone of your voice and body language is more important than the actual sanction itself. Your tone must be clear, firm and formal.

Aggression in the classroom

"His face was really red and I thought he was going to hit me. I was off on sick leave for a long time after that incident and my confidence has taken a dive."

Be prepared for the rare possibility of aggression directed to you by taking appropriate training.

Sometimes, a situation can flare up and students can turn their aggression directly at you. It is obviously a frightening moment. One of the best things you can do is to practise how you would respond if such a situation arose.

A good way to do this is to get together with a group of colleagues and work out appropriate 'what if' role play scenarios.

Learn how to use your voice, choose appropriate verbal language, body language and hand gestures to firmly and calmly de-escalate the situation. Practise with your colleagues. In fact, it is only through practise that you learn how best to deal with such high-stress situations.

You will find that you have to pitch your response carefully. If you act too submissively you can encourage an assault. Be too firm and that too can cause an escalation.

In order to stack the probability of a satisfactory outcome in your favour, prior training is a must. Hopefully, you will never need to use it, but the training will give you an important edge and give you some measure of confidence to take control when necessary.

Teaching tip

If you have the opportunity, go on a professional training course that will help you to deal with such matters in more detail, giving you the behaviour management skills to put you back in control.

Only target the ringleaders

"I worked hard all lesson and then I got kept back for trouble caused by someone else. I might as well join in and cause trouble instead of working. I'd be no worse off!"

It's not fair to punish innocent students.

When a teacher has had a tough lesson it is tempting for him to take it out on the whole class by keeping the whole group after school for an impromptu short detention. It is always a mistake to punish those who have done nothing wrong. It causes the flowing problems:

- Parents can complain.
- Good behaviour is discouraged.
- Ringleaders can hide behind the whole group.
- It is extremely difficult to manage a challenging group after school (friends may be making faces at doors, pushing into the room.)

Quite simply, you must discern who the troublemakers are and let them know that their actions will have consequences.

It is not an exact science but in a challenging class of say 25-30 students you will usually find that roughly five or six students will cause most of the trouble. Half of the rest of the class will behave really well and the remaining students will behave if the overall discipline is good but unfortunately, they will swing towards the disruptors if the disruptors gain any ground.

It is important for the teacher to understand 'the balance of power' that takes place in a classroom and this is why the ringleaders must be identified, made aware that you are watching them and know that they will be dealt with (though not necessarily there and then).

Less marking, more managing

"I'm so exhausted doing all the things expected of me, and work so late at night, I don't feel I've got the energy and I'm dreading dealing with that difficult group tomorrow."

Dealing with behaviour management requires a lot of energy. Marking is one of the biggest drains on a teacher's energy.

To become efficient with behaviour management you need to free up as much time and energy as possible to deal with it.

Any subject has marking patterns which repeat the same sorts of comments. Obviously, not *all* comments are repeated but a large proportion of them are.

A great way to save yourself time is to produce your own stickers. Programme your computer to print text onto the stickers and prepare sets of them containing the comments you use most regularly. Make sure that these comments are clear. Then, when you are marking you simply have to affix the appropriate sticker. Examples of comments to put on stickers include:

- 'Please use a dictionary to check the words I've highlighted.'
- 'You need to support the point you're making with an example, please.'
- 'Please write this out more neatly.'

You will find after that the initial investment of time making the stickers you will be set up with a great time-saving resource.

- The student's books look neater and more professional.
- Students will be able to read your comments easily, saving you from interpreting them during class.

Teaching tip

Colour code the types of comments and see if you can get colleagues in your department to produce similar stickers so that you can share and benefit from the economies of scale.

The second timetable

"I thought that behaviour management was just about managing students. I now realise it also about managing myself and the most important part of that is using my time well."

Create a second timetable and stick to it. This idea will help you to manage your workload and use your time efficiently.

Many teachers find they cannot cope with the enormous amount of tasks imposed on them, and then end up working all hours until the job is done. In the long run this will wear you down.

To put you back in control, design a second timetable. List all the jobs you have to do and allocate each task to a specific time. For example:

- Mondays 4-5pm: Mark Year 8 exercise books.
- Tuesdays 4-5pm: Reply to all emails and complete admin folder.
- Wednesdays 6-7pm: Plan lessons for next week.

If you stick to your timetable you will find that you worry less about your work, since you know that all tasks are allocated then all your energy can be spent on teaching. You will find that you have more free time to rest. In fact, allocate rest time into your timetable.

Of course, you cannot predict every task that you will have to do so it is also important to build in time for the unexpected tasks.

Don't let students cross the line

"I know I went too far. Fair enough. It's alright now."

Make sure that you clearly establish a minimum behaviour expectation that is never crossed.

Some teachers make so many allowances for their challenging students that they forget about the other students who do not misbehave.

The best solution is to use all possible strategies to include difficult students. Try to be like a referee who does not pick up every little thing because he wants there to be flow in the game. You must have a 'line' and make sure your students know not to cross it.

There are times when despite your fair and professional approach, a student disregards it all and does whatever he wants to. This is where you can bring in a senior member of staff for a special meeting. Explain very clearly, and in great detail, the strategies you have used and show how reasonable you have been. Also provide an account of the student's behaviour which is so clearly unacceptable.

There may well be something in the student's personal life that has contributed to their poor behaviour. But in practice, clearly explaining why you are annoyed and showing that the 'line' has been crossed, may be enough for the student to realise that he's gone too far and you will see them try to change their behaviour for the better.

Teaching tip

Remember you can show annoyance, after all, you are only human, but that doesn't stop you from being friendly, professional and caring. Although it's basic, remember also that it's the behaviour you're annoyed at, not the student.

I was partly to blame

"The effect it had was amazing. It seemed to work on their behaviour like magic!"

By accepting some of the blame for a bad lesson your students will see you as fair and will see your strong commitment and determination for getting it right next time.

Teaching tip

Be careful to only use this idea sparingly and with classes you have built a working relationship with. The point is that when you acknowledge some of the blame, then change the work a little, and that in itself goes a long way to bringing about the behaviour you desire.

It takes courage and experience to actually say to the class that you were partly to blame for the terrible behaviour last lesson. But, if you do can do this – carefully – it can be a very powerful tool.

If you are in the habit of analysing what went wrong in a bad lesson then you usually find that it is a combination of poor behaviour *and* work which is sometimes not that interesting to your students, delivered in a flat, unstimulating way. One problem fuels another.

Begin the lesson by outlining what went wrong in the last lesson. Say something like: 'Now it's quite clear that some of you were behaving in a way that was totally unacceptable. However, I'm prepared to admit that I'm partly to blame. I've looked at the work I set you and maybe it was a little tricky and some parts were confusing.' Explain clearly and quickly what you have done to try to put this right. For instance, that you have re-written the worksheets and added some help sheets.

Then say, encouragingly, 'Now, with these improved worksheets and your improved behaviour, I feel sure that'll we'll have a much better lesson today. Don't you?'

Small improvements

"The reason this works for me is that it creates a dialogue of praise rather than reprimand."

Keep a record of small improvements and good things you've spotted and give students feedback on these privately.

Everyone likes to think, with pride, that they're building up a good track record. However, for many students who have low self-esteem and behavioural problems, their track record might not be one to be proud of. Certainly, they wouldn't want it recorded or publicly displayed.

'The private track record' is a simple system. Keep a special notebook, dedicating a page to each student where you can record comments and notes about their work. The notes should be brief, encouraging and positive.

Examples of notes I have made:

- Jack entered the room much more settled.
- Rumya scribbled far less in her exercise book.
- Daktari called out far less and put his hand up more.
- Natalie was on time for class four out of five times this week.

The best time to show a student their page is after the lesson, almost as a casual comment. Keep the feedback brief and upbeat.

The value of this idea is that it shows the student that good behaviour is noticed and rewarded and it also gives you the opportunity to praise a student that you find yourself frequently reprimanding.

Teaching tip

As you build up more and more positive comments ask students if you may show the book to the headteacher. This small action will boost their self-esteem greatly. It really helps if you can get other staff to help you praise students for these small improvements, or to do use the same notebooks in their classes.

The classroom setting

"I've noticed that class 9C behaves badly in the untidy History room but they behave well in the orderly Geography room. I wonder why that is?"

How you set up, organise and manage your teaching space has a huge impact on your behaviour management.

The following guidelines for classroom layout are vital:

- Make sure challenging students are all facing you. If students are put into small group layouts the teacher cannot observe them.
- If the class is small enough, put one student to each double desk.
- Keep known troublemakers well apart.
- Have space between desks so that you can move around the room. This will give you a huge psychological advantage as it breaks down barriers. An impenetrable cluster of desks that you can't get near sets up a 'them vs you' mentality. It also means that you can observe students from the back of the room and not just the front.
- Make sure that there is ample space between you and the front desks. This gives you space to move about freely, confidently and comfortably when you teach and demonstrate. Teachers often underestimate, or ignore altogether the value of this territory.
- Make sure you have easy access to cupboards, projectors, electronic white boards and any other resources.
- A simple but effective way to model your high standards to the class is to keep your own desk and materials neat and tidy.

Bring lessons to life

"He's a great teacher! I love the way he says things!"

Use positive language and be creative in the way you describe things.

Words and how you use them have a powerful effect on your students. Certain words trigger certain responses. If you say: 'Come into the classroom' even the word 'classroom' can have a negative connotation and lower the mood at a subconscious level. If you say instead 'Enter this temple of learning' you will create a more positive feeling about what is happening. Don't say: 'We're going to have a test today', instead say: 'We now have a great opportunity to present what we've learned.'

The more you think about and experiment with the words you use in your lessons the more you can bring them alive and make them seem more fun, friendly and interesting.

Even a simple thing like: 'I'm going to show you all a picture of...' can sound boring. Why not build it up a bit and say something like: 'In a moment I want to show you something that for millions of years mankind never, ever saw!' Then show them a picture of the earth seen from space.

When delivered with a cheerful, positive upbeat style this way of describing things adds fun to your lessons and the students love it. Your students may criticise what you say but persist and eventually they too will use a more positive language.

I didn't realise quite how effective this idea was until I was away from one of my lessons and a cover teacher told me that ten minutes before the end of the lesson students started to demand their 'world-famous plenary!'

Teaching tip

Keep using creative language it until it becomes a habit. You will find that it reduces tension, engages students and that, overall, your classes are a bit more fun!

Taking it further

Challenge yourself to use a different unusual word in every lesson! Perhaps even get your students to suggest words for you to use in the next lesson and then you can report back about how you managed it.

The book of wind ups

"Since using this book my mood has improved. I can stay calm in the face of any wind up!"

By anticipating and recording wind ups you will lessen their impact.

Most teachers, at any given time, are 'wound up' by something. Teaching is a high-risk profession for stress and the wind ups come from a huge variety of sources. Maybe a student has been particularly obnoxious; maybe the worksheets you spent hours preparing have been chucked onto the floor; maybe a colleague has been offhand with you.

When faced with students with challenging behaviour you need all the energy and mental resilience you can get and having to deal with wind ups is incredibly draining. It is not the wind up itself that causes the problem but your reaction to them that really matters. The simplest and most effective method for dealing with wind ups is to expect them! And the best way to do this is to keep a record of them by jotting them down in a small notebook. Obviously, for practical reasons, you shouldn't record every single little irritation, but do jot down the ones that come up a lot.

This takes the edge out of any wind up because you turn the whole thing into a sort of game. Supposing you have a list of wind ups, numbered from 1 to 7, in your notebook for that day. You will gradually realise that wind ups are a just part of teaching. You are never going to have a single day without them so you might as well deal with them in a way that gives you back control.

Teacher-student tennis

"I like my teacher. He never really gets rattled, no matter what you say. He gets you working."

Use banter to manage behaviour and inspire a positive frame of mind.

With experience, you will realise the way you use language is crucial to controlling behaviour. There is a sort of sub-group of language skills used in a classroom, a sort of teacher-student 'tennis' banter, which is of vital importance. In fact, I have never seen a great teacher who doesn't use it!

At its heart it is the way a teacher reframes students' comments to turn negative comments into positive ones. It is like tennis because the student serves you a tricky ball and you return it with rhythm and pace.

So, for example, a student may say: 'This work is boring!' A suitable comment back might be: 'Well Sophie, how can we make this more interesting for you today then?'

The great things about this technique are that it:

- Avoids conflict.
- Keeps the pace going.
- Lightens the mood.
- Deflects the flow of energy in a useful way.
- Engenders a positive habit of response in the teacher.
- Reduces, over time, the negative attitudes of the students and encourages them into a more positive frame of mind. Positive banter is infectious!

Teaching tip

As you become more used to this technique you can praise the students for their comments in a careful way, praising them for a good 'serve' and then return the 'ball', with 'spin' on it, to get them thinking. For example: if a student says: 'I can't do this! There's too much to read!' reply with: 'Good observation Harry! Well done. You could be right. How could we break this up into smaller chunks to make it more manageable?'

Engage their interests

"Generally speaking, people don't do well if you tell them to do something. It's much better if they *want* to do it."

Find out what the students are interested in and try to make connections to their work to engage them in your lesson.

Build up, over time, knowledge of what students really love and have a passion for. You can pick this up from casual conversations with students. Make notes about their interests, which football teams they like and which celebrities are popular, and keep it in mind when trying to engage students in a topic or activity that they are unwilling or reluctant to complete.

For example, you might have a student who is pushing his work to one side in a technology class. The purpose of the lesson is to design a new type of chair but he simply isn't interested. He can't see the point and he's in a bad mood.

But you happen to know that this student is a big fan of singer Beyoncé. So encourage him to think about the type of chair that Beyoncé might like. Try to cheer him up, put enthusiasm into your voice and say: 'Hey, Charlie, what if you won a competition to design a chair for Beyoncé? What would that chair look like?'

Talking in terms of their interests and creatively linking it to the work can often act as a tipping point in persuading them to start working.

Cue the music

"I used to stand there shouting and they just ignored me. A music cue is a much better idea. It is a very powerful and enjoyable trigger."

Use a music cue to get students' attention.

Getting the students to listen to you at the start of a lesson and at key points during the lesson can often be tiring and tedious. This idea will make it fun and effective and easier.

Have a CD player ready and play a few seconds of music quite loudly. Then turn the volume down and say: 'Now that has got to be better than shouting!' Then go straight into your presentation. If you find that some students are still talking after the music cue, say: 'Oh dear! Most people responded beautifully to the music cue. One more time and...' Play the music again, then pause it again and you will find it works like magic and you will get their attention.

Once the idea is established and running with your classes it can make it more fun if they bring in their own favourite music to play as a cue.

Bonus idea

Another great way to get their attention using recorded sounds is to play mystery sounds. You play the sound and then pause it and ask: 'Can anybody tell me what that sound is?' It might, for example, be a key turning in a lock or water running down a bath plughole. To avoid everybody shouting out together insist that they must always put their hand up to answer or you will not accept their answer. If they can't guess it, a great way to hold their attention is to give them a clue and play it again. You will find that the students love the game and will ask if they can play again later in the lesson. Of course, if you can link the mystery sounds to the content of the lesson then it works even better!

Parables

"I was out of order and he did make his point very well without making me feel bad."

Use this idea to make your point very clear without constantly reprimanding students.

As a teacher you are not just teaching your subject. You are teaching your students how to be good citizens. When it comes to life skills, when you see examples of bad behaviour you can use them as an opportunity to tell an eccentric parable. They make it clear as to why good behaviour is important without it being yet another reprimand.

For example, one of the most common forms of poor behaviour is a lack of patience. Perhaps a student is asking for her exercise book and as you search for it she demands it in a loud and unpleasant way. Tell her about the rich man in the very posh hotel who rang for champagne and caviar to be brought to his room 'right now!' The waiter replied that he would bring it up 'straight away' to which the rich man shouted: 'Are you deaf or stupid? I said I want it now!' The guest was asked to leave the hotel because the manager would simply not tolerate such impatience.

You can then point out to the student that surely they are nicer than that? Encourage the student, and the whole class, to have more patience.

With experience you can build up a surprisingly large range of stories and fables to match other examples of poor behaviour. I try to present them in a lively and entertaining way but the message which underlies them is serious.

Bonus idea ★

It is also a good idea to have display inspirational pictures alongside short inspirational quotes. Then, when you need to draw someone's attention to poor behaviour you can point to the quote. Referring to them frequently will really emphasise your point.

An end of lesson treat

"I love the bit at the end of the lesson where we do something different and fun. It's my favourite part of the day!"

By having five minutes of fun at the end of a lesson it motivates the students to work hard all through the lesson.

Planning a short but fun activity for the end of a lesson is not only very effective but also popular with students. The five-minutes of fun are offered as a reward at the end of the lesson on the condition that students behave well and complete the work you set them. The activity should be something totally different from the lesson. There is a wide range of fun activities but here are a few examples:

- Project an optical illusion.
- Show an extreme close-up of an everyday object up and see if they can guess what it is.
- Give an amazing fact for example, Vincent Van Gogh died in poverty but a lottery jackpot would not buy one of his paintings today.
- Tell a funny story.

I also invite students to come to the front to demonstrate or present something. Here are some of the popular types of things:

- Sing a song.
- Act a mime.
- Play 'Which is false?' (Give three facts about themselves, one of which is false, and the others have to guess which one).

This activity should only be used when your lesson has been completed or when all students have finished their work. Only when everything is cleared away and packed up and the class are ready to finish should you allow the five-minute activity to start.

Teaching tip

Don't forget to use the 'promise' of the session as you progress through the lesson to encourage good behaviour, say things like 'Oh, we're not making the progress we should. At this rate we won't be able to fit in our fun activity at the end of class.' It is a very powerful technique to motivate students.